The Art of the DEAL: GOLF- Access to Success

Art of the DEAL: GOLF- Access to Success

ROSE HARPER

Foreword by SHEILA C. JOHNSON

THE
GRASS
CEILING
INC.

WASHINGTON, DC

Cover and interior design by Bruce Boyd.
Cover photograph: Rose Harper on the tee at The Crosby Invitational. Winston-Salem, NC. Photographer Unknown.

For permission requests, write to the publisher, addressed "Attention: Permissions Coordinator," at the address below:
The Grass Ceiling, Inc.
P.O. Box 5874
Washington, DC 20016
www.thegrassceiling.com

The syllabus of the program *The Art of the Deal: Golf–Access to Success* was approved for Continuing Education credits by Howard University Continuing Education, a unit that was certified by the International Association for Continuing Education and Training (IACET).

Ordering Information:
Special discounts are available on quantity purchases by corporations, associations, college and universities and others. For details, contact the Grass Ceiling / Rose Harper Leadership Academy Special Sales.

Phone: (202) 966-5622; Fax: (202) 966-5623
Email: grassc@aol.com; Website: www.thegrassceiling.com

Library of Congress Publisher's Cataloging-in-Publication Data

Harper, Rose.
    Art of the Deal Golf: Access to Success / Rose Harper.—1st ed.
      p. cm.
    ISBN 978-0-9903962-0-8
    1. Business   2. Golf   3. Leadership Development/Diversity &
Library of Congress control number   2014913524
Published by Rose Harper Leadership Academy

First Edition

Printed in the United States of America

10 9 8 7 6 5 4 3 2 1

This book is dedicated to...

To those whose shoulders I stand. Building on their legacy and magnifying their dreams, as they continue to fuel my thoughts and commitments to continue their work to provide equal access, especially for all women and minorities in this wonderful world of golf.

I am blessed to be the beneficiary of their sacrifices!

To my family and friends who continue to support me and my work, and love me unconditionally, and to those dear family members and friends who have left this world way too soon.

And especially to my South African brother, Peter K.O.P. Matseke.

SHEILA C. JOHNSON
Chief Executive Officer,
Salamander Hotels and Resorts.

FOREWORD
by Sheila C. Johnson

❧

I f you had told me ten years ago that I would one day own nine golf courses and sit on the executive committee of the United States Golf Association, I would have said you were crazy. I was no one's definition of a golf enthusiast. I had never even played a single round! What's more, I thought of golf as a sport dominated by middle-aged white men—not a sport for people like me.

Then, in 2007, I was offered the chance to purchase the Innisbrook Golf Resort and Spa near Tampa Bay, Florida. I fell in love with this historic property, so I decided to go for it. I invested in major renovations. I hired Rodney Green—one of only 85 African Americans among the 27,000 PGA professionals—to serve as the resort's director of golf. And I also decided that it was finally time for me to pick up a set of clubs and sign up for golf lessons.

When my good friend former Secretary of State Condoleezza Rice came to Innisbrook to visit, she invited me to play my very first 18-hole round. I'd be lying if I said I found it easy—especially when we went out again the next day, and it started pouring rain. But I had a great time. So I stuck with my lessons, and I've seen a steady improvement. Being out on the links is a wonderful way to enjoy the outdoors with my friends.

While neither Condi nor I grew up playing golf, the fact that we've both grown to love the sport is one more piece of evidence that the face of golf is changing. Unfortunately, in many people's minds, golf remains an exclusive, elite pastime—an "old boys' club" with a closed door. When I purchased Innisbrook, I heard from many people—especially women and African Americans—who told me that even though they had a deep interest in golf, they had never felt like the sport was open to them. To my mind, that's a terrible loss— for them, and for the sport.

I understand why so many people, particularly women and minorities, still feel uncomfortable, intimidated, or alienated by golf—and I strongly believe it's time for that to change. In my own experience, I've seen that golf is so much more than just a sport: It's an extension of the boardroom, a setting for important business discussions, and a way to forge connections and deepen professional relationships. Important things are taking place on the links, and everyone should be a part of them. That includes you!

Today, as the owner of the Grand Golf Resorts of Florida and the first African American woman to sit on the U.S.G.A's executive committee, I'm determined to make golf more accessible and welcoming to all. I spend a lot of time thinking about how to recruit a new, more diverse range of golf enthusiasts—including women, minorities, youth, and the disabled. I want more people to have the opportunity to take advantage of all that golf has to offer.

This important book is a wonderful resource to encourage people of all backgrounds to step off the sidelines and onto the green. My friend Rose Harper has seen firsthand that there is so much you can learn, contribute, and achieve on the golf course—and she has devoted her career to making sure that women and minorities are empowered to access those benefits as well. Not only does this book cover the basics of the sport, it also offers practical advice and insider tips to leave you feeling confident and ready for tee time.

As you begin exploring the exciting world of golf, remember that from the U.S.G.A. to The Grass Ceiling, there are so many people behind you—and all of us are rooting for you.

ACKNOWLEDGMENTS

For all whose fingerprints are on this book, and I have had an enormous amount of help, I offer my sincere thanks for your contributions in getting this book published.

To my friend, Tony Regusters, who helped me move my three years of working notes into reality by beginning the initial editing process to get this book off the ground, conducting interviews, editing and giving voice to the testimonials;

For all of you who have attended my *The Art of the Deal: Golf-Access to Success* workshop/seminars and continued to request and encouraged me to write the book, I thank you for your support;

For all of my friends and supporters who helped launch our first seminar in 2000:

> To my dear friend Kathryn Crosby who came as our special guest,

> To The Honorable Sheila Sisulu (former Ambassador to the United States from South Africa) for her support in convening all of her female peers,

> To Arch Campbell (NBC) who thought our program had merit enough to cover it,

> To Peter Kulsziski, Sanddollar Productions, for providing video documentation; and

To Joe Hardy, who generously sponsored one of my first seminars,

To my friends, John and Nadine Daniel, who bought me a tape recorder, 3x5 cards and monthly phone calls of encouragement and profound words of wisdom;

To Maxine LeGall and Nancy Owens who met with me monthly every Wednesday to develop the syllabus for the workshop/ seminars, and to Dr. Peggy Berry for facilitating the certification of our workshops;

To my friend Bruce Boyd, an extraordinary talented and gifted graphic designer who has taken our written words and made them come alive on the pages of this book;

To my dear friends Q.T. Jackson and Maxine LeGall, the editorial specialist, who came in to help give this book shape and focus and to finish this book "under-par;" and to Giselle Denbow our editorial assistant.

And to all those individuals who provided testimonials in support of *The Art of the Deal: Golf–Access to Success* workshop/seminars, I offer my deep and heartfelt thanks.

Finally, to my brother K.O.P. Matseke (Peter), my extreme gratitude without his support this book would not have been possible.

Rose Harper

"If you teach, you have to live your teaching."—Maya Angelou

CONTENTS

INTRODUCTION

❦

I grew up in Pleasantville, New Jersey, a small town just outside of Atlantic City. During the fifties and early sixties, it was a rite of passage for the teenage boys to work as caddies at either the Atlantic City Country Club or the Seaview Country Club. During those summers, I learned the game from the ground up from seasoned caddies, some of whom caddied for professional golfers on the PGA tour. In retrospect, what I saw as a teenager's dream summer job, I now see as an introduction to a dynamic sport that has reverberated throughout my personal and professional life.

Rose Harper leading one of *The Art of the Deal: Golf–Access to Success* workshop/seminar.

Fast forward twenty-five years. I am an educator working in a sports management office as Program Manager, and Rose Harper is the founder and executive director. Working as her employee, I was assigned to assist with the preparation and implementation of our office's legendary Annual Golf Pro-Am Tournament. During this time, I learned about the planning that goes into hosting a major event, and how to successfully manage the multiple details that had to be developed and coordinated. At first, like most people, I was impressed by the long and distinguished list of celebrities from every profession and every career field that participated in the Tournament. Against this backdrop, one part of the event stood out: Rose's attention to the education of the young people assigned to work in each division of the tournament. They had jobs and they were required to attend lectures delivered by people Rose had invited to speak to them about their future careers, about the training they would need in the world of work, and about the career opportunities in the golf and sports industry.

Using an extension of this model, in 1988 Rose took the first African American youth delegation to the Olympics to study the behind-the-scene business of conducting the largest sporting event in the world. Rose led our delegation of ten: two high school seniors, five college students, an NBC-Channel 4 Network cameraman and me, a mentor/chaperone. The

Rose Harper presents the official gift from the city of Washington, D.C. to the Director of the Seoul Olympic Organizing Committee.

Seoul Olympic Organizing Committee had accepted our Sports Management Institutes' proposal on its merits and invited us to attend the Olympics as their guests after personally meeting with Rose in Korea, three months prior to the games. We were housed in the Olympic Village along with the participating athletes, coaches, officials, and delegates. Rose served as a U.S. Delegate, and attended the daily briefing sessions of delegates from 52 countries. Our youth delegates were covering events, interviewing Olympic officials, Olympians, and celebrities. They gave live news broadcasts from Korea to WOL Radio with Kathy Hughes, on the popular radio station in Washington, D.C. They understood that they were there to learn, to work, and then to have fun. On one memorable day, when each delegation was required to make a presentation, they gave a performance of Michael Jackson's "We are the World." As youth from around the world stood and enthusiastically joined in, we experienced the global village first hand!

During our stay, we had the opportunity to introduce and promote to the other delegates and the 952 young people from around the

Rose Harper and a member of the 1988 Seoul Olympic Organizing Committee with members of the U.S. African American Youth Delegation. (Not shown-three youth of the camera crew.)

world the concept that golf, like other sports, should be played in the Olympic Games. Now in 2014, we are excited that a golf course is currently under construction in Brazil, the host country for the 2016 Olympic Games where golf will be played as an Olympic sport for the first time!

I saw Rose work to make that trip happen. I saw her develop the plan for our delegation, and her tenacity to raise the funds, to coordinate the travel, to work closely with the Seoul and United States Organizing Olympic Committee officials. I saw her dedication and commitment to our youth and their families. I saw how she used the event and its intricacies to train the youth to understand the many roles needed to implement an event of that magnitude. Needless to say, the trip and the experiences were resounding successes.

Ever the visionary, and with the same intensity and devotion that drove her then, in 2000, Rose developed a vehicle that would serve to introduce women and minorities to the game for its business an empowerment applications. She created The Grass Ceiling, Inc. to sponsor the exposure and empowerment workshop/seminar, *The Art of the Deal: Golf–Access to Success*. As Special Advisor to the Executive Director and member of The Grass Ceiling, Inc., I have learned there are fine points to using the game as a business development tool.

This handbook, a companion to the workshop/seminar, explains in straight forward language what you need to know to utilize the game of golf to generate business and personal success.

The first chapter addresses the new realities of the game and dispels several popular misconceptions associated with golf. Chapter Two provides a quick overview of the game. In Chapter Three, the theory and practice of how golf works as a business development tool is explained through the use of insightful Case Studies from Rose's Playbook.

The next two chapters introduce related concepts of conduct; the importance of playing by the rules and the associated etiquette; and why it is necessary to have the right fitting equipment and dress for the game.

Chapter six reminds players to have fun.

Chapter Seven provides the steps in the process for hosting successful business golf outings. Chapter Eight highlights using golf for leadership development and to promote diversity and inclusion. Chapter Nine completes the front nine by reviewing golf from the stand point of membership.

You can consider this companion handbook your personal caddy before you step onto the course to play business golf.

After reading these nine chapters, you too will see golf as both a game and a tool to promote your business interests on a local and a global scale.

Q.T. Jackson, Jr.

Acclaim for

The Art of the Deal: GOLF–Access to Success

"Golf is a very difficult individual game. It doesn't care if you have great athletic skills; some of the finest athletes cannot play well, and therein lies a question, 'what is playing well?' It's whatever you can achieve, whatever brings you pleasure. It's a lot like life… Golf is access at the highest level… because the game is the same for all of us (the objective unfortunately not the skill level); it's a great leveler… Rose Harper's *The Art of the Deal: Golf–Access to Success* workshop/seminar is an important stepping stone and shows women how to effectively use the game to secure new business opportunities."

—**BARNEY ADAMS,** Founder of Adams Golf and inventor of the Tight Lies Fairway wood

"As a former partner in a large law firm and a former Chief of Staff for a Member of Congress, I know the importance of building relationship. Rose Harper's *The Art of the Deal: Golf–Access to Success* workshop/seminars helps lawyers, executives, and entrepreneurs in the United States and abroad understands how to use the game of golf to build those relationships. Rose is a wonderful teacher. She offers great insight and strategic advice on how to use golf to help professionals with rainmaking, client development, and networking. When I worked with Rose assisting her in negotiating her deal with the Commonwealth of Bermuda to organize a series of local golf tournaments, I saw first-hand that Rose practices what she preaches. I believe that *The Art of the Deal: Golf–Access to Success* handbook is a must have for anyone looking to strengthen or develop long-lasting business relationships."

—**LEAH ALLEN, ESQ**

"Rose is an amazing organizer and her *The Art of the Deal: Golf–Access to Success* workshop/seminar was wonderful and fun! I learned a lot and the group of women was wonderful. Rose presented very important points why golf is such an important game, and her credentials, of course, speak for themselves. I highly recommend *The Art of the Deal: Golf–Access to Success* workshop/seminars was a great opportunity for enjoyment and for networking."

—**DR. ALONA BAUER,** General and Cosmetic Dentistry

"An afternoon of golf is an option offered at the annual Conference of University Business Officers. As business professionals we know the value of golf as a tool for doing business. This is a game that allows peers to meet and exchange ideas in a relaxed setting. Thanks to all that I learned via Rose Harper's *The Art of the Deal: Golf–Access to Success* seminar, I made a point of taking the option to play golf at the conference each year. Realizing I was the sole female in a foursome, I made great use of the time with my peers using Rose's techniques and advice gained in her seminars. When my Senior VP played one year, I found a moment to suggest that he advertise my position. "Where are you going?," he asked. "You're going to promote me!," was my reply, just like a man might have suggested. The very next month, he did exactly that! This was a conversation that may not have happened in the office."

—**A.J. BELL-REID,** Assistant Vice-President (Retired) for Financial Management Howard University

"I've always been a sports fanatic—playing basketball, volleyball, softball, table tennis, and running track from elementary school through college. I took up the game of golf in the middle years of my career and what a difference the game has made in my life! I'm passionate about sports but there is really something special about golf—a point perfectly expressed in Rose Harper's wonderful *The Art of the Deal: Golf–Access to Success* workshop and seminar."

—**MARILYN E. COLE,** Local Government Executive (Retired)

"Rose Harper takes the mystique out of golf and makes it an inviting and accessible game for everyone. By sharing so many insights about the game, she truly supports her strong and well-articulated belief that golf is a universal game and the one reliable place at which recreational and business activity come together. As a former public company CEO, I wish this book had been available long ago to share with women and other groups who wanted to position themselves for higher-level opportunity and for great fun."

—**MICHAEL J. CRITELLI,** Executive Producer,
"From the Rough" Productions

"I have experienced a lot of 'It' moments in my personal life and professional career. I define an 'It' moment as a game changing, examples include meeting and ultimately marrying my husband; making a decision that was the right one, at the right time; a promotion or bonus received that let me know that even though I was unaware, people noticed my sacrifices and work ethic. To my 'It' moments, I unabashedly add meeting Ms. Rose Harper; and participating in her *The Art of the Deal: Golf–Access to Success* workshop/seminar. When I first met Ms. Harper I had been playing golf for approximately two years. After meeting Ms. Harper and taking her seminar, my enhancement of the game was even more elevated. For it was then that I truly gained an appreciation of how important the sport of golf was in developing and enhancing leadership skills. *The Art of the Deal: Golf–Access to Success* workshop/seminar opened my eyes to the fact that I was sitting on a business gold mine that I hadn't realized. The seminar enabled me to understand how effective golf was in terms of not only serving as a valuable networking tool; but also as a vehicle—especially for me as an African American woman—that had the amazing power to tear down racial and gender barriers by leveling the playing field. What a great deal! Ms. Harper's passion, and understanding of the game of golf is on point and awe-inspiring!"

—**V. NADINE DANIEL, JD**

"Unlike most sports, golf expects its Rules to be respected. They are not viewed as burdensome restrictions to the conduct of the game, but rather as a framework in which a competition can proceed fairly. It must be remembered that other sports have a fixed common field with one ball in play for all to see. Golf, on the other hand, can have 150 balls in play at one time over 160 acres of unique topography. Without their being an easy way of monitoring their play, players are expected to call penalties on their fellow competitors and most importantly on themselves. Yes, there are Referees and the Committee; however, the participants themselves provide the first line of scorekeeping. Officials are present to simply assist the player. One of the unique features of golf is the attesting procedure in stroke play where the player, via his/her signature, attests to their score. A game of honor played by honorable people."

—**JERRY DUFFY,** Maryland State Golf Association
Rules Official – Member of the USGA
Senior Amateur Committee

"A powerful message by the true 'Lady of Golf' of how the sport of golf presents a world of opportunity, career enhancement, while providing the self- discipline, and self-improvement we all need in our pursuits… I know Rose Harper as a gracious, super well-organized executive woman and a great golfer. *The Art of the Deal: Golf–Access to Success* workshop/seminars are a great application for women and minorities seeking to benefit from the opportunities the game of golf presents as an effective tool for networking and making successful business connections. Most golfers look at other golfers and see peers, and all the barriers come down. The game of golf instills great self-confidence, and will empower and enrich you. You will benefit greatly from a powerful message by the true 'Lady of Golf.'"

—**ED DWIGHT,** Former NASA Astronaut, Owner,
Ed Dwight Studios, Inc.

"Rose Harper is a respected voice, role model and pioneer in women's golf who has worked tirelessly to advance the game. Rose's *The Art of the Deal: Golf–Access to Success* workshops are an invaluable tool to help women navigate the intersecting worlds of golf and business. Rose unlocks the magic that golf has as an instrument to help advance women's careers and understanding the role golf has in the business world."

—CARMEN GUZMAN, ESQ

"Golf has always been an important factor in my personal and business life. Golf is a great way to get to know someone you may want to do business with, as well meet new prospects in business. The way one shows themselves on the golf course can give insight into who they are as a person. If someone has a bad temper when a shot does not go their way or bends the rules in order to gain an advantage for a shot, that reflects what type of person they may be when having a business relationship.

Having a program to help people use golf to connect on a business level is important. It will give those people more advantages in networking, which is a very important aspect of conducting business. Being an entrepreneur myself, I know firsthand the importance of being able to gain any advantage in the business world and what it has done for me in my successes.

Programs that teach the importance of connecting golf with business, such as Rose Harper's, *The Art of the Deal: Golf–Access to Success*, is a great way for executives to understand how to utilize a great game with great business."

—JOSEPH A. HARDY, CEO, 84 Lumber

"*The Art of the Deal: Golf–Access to Success* is an excellent tool for diversity and inclusion strategy. Rose Harper, with eloquence, style, and a unique insider perspective; teaches the game of golf as… a path of entry into the inner circles where decisions and deals are done. Corporate Diversity officers should give this book to every participant in their executive leadership development program."

—**MARYANNE HOWLAND,** President & CEO, Ibis Communications
and Founder & CEO, Global Diversity
Leadership Exchange

"Hughes Capital Management, Inc., is a minority/woman-owned firm that manages $1 billion in assets. Several of our clients host annual golf tournaments for which my firm has participated as a sponsor. Having a very good appreciation for the importance of golf as a networking instrument, I attended Rose Harper's *The Art of the Deal: Golf–Access to Success* workshop/seminar and came away with greater insights about how to position our sponsorships, support our clients, and advance our company's goals. This business seminar was a great ROI for Hughes Capital Management—and for me personally—as I look forward to spending more time on the golf course with my clients in the future."

—**FRANKIE HUGHES,** President & Chief Investment Officer
Hughes Capital Management

Rose Harper's *The Art of the Deal: Golf–Access to Success* book is "A welcomed contribution to the body of work informing people *how to get it done* in the business world. It is helpful to the reader that it is presented by a woman of grace, class and style. She has extensive experience in this area of tremendous interest to all who want to get into the *game* of making the right connections."

—**ATTY RONALD C. JESSAMY, PLLC**

"As an entrepreneur, my decision to start playing golf gave me the opportunity to network with many in the business world that I might not have met otherwise. As a business tool, golf can't be beat. I highly recommend Rose Harper's *The Art of the Deal: Golf–Access to Success* workshop/seminars as an effective way to understand and effectively use the game and benefit from it..."

—**LILLIAN LINCOLN LAMBERT,** LilCo, Enterprises, Inc.

20 years ago, my husband an avid golfer, and I were business partners. I soon realized that many of the deals what were cut in our business occurred after 18 holes of golf, and were closed during the '19th hole' of roundtable discussions in the club house. I wasn't a golfer and therefore found myself excluded from the deal-making opportunities that were generated by the bonding made on the course. I therefore decided that it was important that I too be seen as an equal partner, fully capable of participating in 'the art of the deal'. I became a serious student of the game. The game of golf has opened many doors that never would have been opened had I merely stayed behind the desk, working behind the scenes. As my friend Rose Harper tells you in *The Art of the Deal: Golf–Access to Success*, it is essential that you make the game part of your strategy for professional growth and development. Be a participant in the art of the deal, not merely the conduit for implementation once the deal is cut. I guarantee that you will make personal and professional memories that will be with you forever.

—**DIANA RILEY,** Founder, Swinging With Purpose

"*The Art of the Deal: Golf–Access to Success* workshop/seminars have been a very important teaching tool for me in my growth and development in the professional golf industry. It has been a critical element in my role as part of a successful, female-owned, golf management company. Ms. Harper and *The Art of the Deal: Golf–Access to Success* has truly contributed to my success. There is no other entity like her workshop/seminars around. No other seminar I've attended by any of the professional golf organizations compare to *The Art of the Deal: Golf–Access to Success* workshop/seminars. Ms. Harper has been and continues to be the driving force with the tenacity and fortitude to educate women about themselves and how to succeed."

—**MARIAN BUCK STALLWORTH,** Vice President, SydMar Golf and Sports Management, Inc.

"This outstanding book, *The Art of the Deal: Golf–Access to Success*, needed to be written to serve women, especially women of color and those who are seeking ways to be more effective in business. It provides a well-spring of knowledge… that can serve to elevate women across a vast array of careers."

—**DR CATANA R. STARKS,** Featured in the movie, "From the Rough"

Golf has given me the opportunity to meet many individuals from all walks of life all around the world. Golf has also allowed me to meet some of golf's living legends—James Black, Charlie Sifford, and Rose Harper—to name a few and to learn about their early struggles for equality on the PGA Tour. Golf has enabled me to successfully network. After being laid off, I was able to meet and network with other computer professionals on the golf course, distribute my resume, and eventually land a job. Above all, through golf I have learned about character: the person that chests on the golf course is the same person that will cheat in the business world.

—**TIM TAYLOR,** Soft wear Engineer, General Dynamics

The path of executive leadership, although incredibly rewarding, can be a difficult and tumultuous journey. Along the way, we must acquire tools to help cultivate our success, build our networks and maintain our sanity! A critical tool along these lines is *The Art of the Deal: Golf–Access to Success*, which details 'must know' information that can only enhance the professional experiences of women in leadership. From Tea time to TEE time, women are embracing leadership roles and realize that leadership, networking and closing deals does not always (or usually) occur within the confines of four walls. With the advice in Rose Harper's book, we can hit the greens equipped to benefit from the full use of the game.

—**Dr Traki L. Taylor,** Dean and Professor- College of Education, Bowie State University

Rose Harper shreds the image of golf as a man's game in which high-powered business deals belonging exclusively to the privileged male world are executed out of sight of women and minorities. Today, women and minorities have a place on the golf course, and in those business dealings just as much as our male counterparts. But like any game, you need to know how to be a player. *The Art of the Deal: Golf -Access to Success* lays out everything a newly minted woman golfer needs to know to play both the fairways and the greens, while using golf to climb the corporate ladder of success. Remember, before you show up at the links, there is much to know, and *The Art of the Deal: Golf–Access to Success* is the one read that will let you in on both the rules and etiquette of the game of golf, while covering everything from how to dress to how to use golf as an effective business tool, and at the same time keeping the game in proper perspective.

As my professional friend and colleague makes clear, golf is meant to be fun, and keep on mind that it is simply an outlet and not your day job. So, if you want to hit them straight, or relatively so, while enjoying yourself in the great outdoors with a sand wedge in your hands, along with giving your career a boost, I highly recommend Rose Harper's *The Art of the Deal: Golf–Access to Success.*"

—**Linda Hitt Thatcher,** Esq, Thatcher Law Firm, LLC

"*The Art of the Deal: Golf–Access to Success* workshop/seminar is one of the most useful tools for female (and other) executives in terms of learning how to use the game of golf to enhance and promote career goals and objectives. The workshop provides a rare opportunity to experience firsthand the wealth of knowledge Rose Harper brings to the business world, including: Inside Tips, mastering 'Old Boy' networking strategies; Dressing for Success (and not duress) on the Course, and moving from the board room to the country club… This seminar is a must for professional's intent on upping their game…"

—**DORA THOMAS,** Procurement Analyst U.S Securities
& Exchange Commission (Retired)

"In my role as an engineer at Hewlett Packard I often make presentations to corporate executives and I find myself leaning on knowledge I've mined from Rose Harper's *The Art of the Deal: Golf–Access to Success* seminars. The love I have for this game and the way golf has enhanced my personal and professional life is nothing short of remarkable. The wisdom, knowledge and confidence I've gained by working with Rose Harper has elevated my success to another level. I cannot recommend a better workshop/seminar anywhere. These seminars and workshops are the best in the business."

—**EARL WEST,** Data Center Engineer,
Hewlett Packard

"What I do know is that golf, especially for executive women, is far too important to allow frustrations to curtail a program that holds any promise whatever of breaking through the glass ceiling."

—**COSMO WILLIAMS,** Managing Director, Carambola Golf Club,
St. Croix, U.S. Virgin Islands

"Rose Harper has demonstrated vision and a pioneering spirit as the first Black female to have a contract with the U.S. Interior Department to manage a public golf course in the nation's capital for the National Park Service, and as the founder, producer, director of a national minority-owned Celebrity Pro Am Golf Tournament, hosting PGA professionals. Now, she's sharing the wealth of her vast experience as a sports management professional, international businesswoman, and golfer with *The Art of the Deal: Golf–Access to Success* workshops and seminars. The business community benefits tremendously from the game of golf, which is a major component of high-level business and political culture. Her workshops develop unique leadership and astounding networking opportunities."

—WILLIE WILLIAMS, WW II, LLC

"Rose knows access. She's built an amazing career getting it and building it. However, Rose is extremely generous in using access to advocate for others. Rose presented to over 100 women at our leadership series on the topic: 'How Women Can Become Their Own Best Advocates' and shared real examples of making a difference where and when you can. I can't wait to read her book— since its all part of building relationships!"

—JUDITH WILSON, Founder & CEO,
Washington Women's Weekly,
LLC

"Imagine every child having the opportunity to learn and experience, not only the game of golf, but also the business of golf—both the art of leveraging golf as a bridge to success, and the science of the enterprise itself, with its myriad of industries and professional paths therein contained. Rose Harper and I have had many dynamic brainstorming conversations regarding ways to universalize the incredible character, college, career, and citizenship-building catalyst that the game of golf represents. What if we could invert the *'access paradigm'* so that golf was ubiquitous, as basketball or soccer are, in the backyards, neighborhoods, and schools of today's young people regardless of geographic, ethnic, or socio-economic background? How much more deeply would the univeral ideals of respect, relationship, reliability, and resilience be woven into the fabric of our global society? In the spirit of this pursuit, Rose Harper is a dearest kinswoman to me, and an indefatigable champion for the present and future multitudes of beneficiaries of her love, her life, and her legacy."

—**MUBUSO ZAMCHIYA,** CEO, Albany Charter School Network

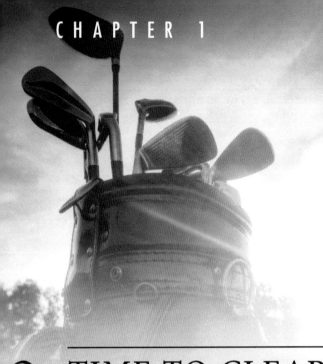

CHAPTER 1

ᔫTIME TO CLEAR THE AIR

Addressing the new realities and dispelling misconceptions of the game

T hings are changing and you can be part of the change. Having the ability to play the game of golf gives you a competitive edge in a concept of advanced business networking that I call, "The Art of the Deal–Golf: Access To Success," which focuses on the ways golf can be used to create a successful atmosphere for networking and building relationships that ultimately lead to doing business.

For years golf has been a game to which women and minorities have had limited access by custom and law. The history and culture of male domination and racial segregation and discrimination have provided a mountainous terrain for women and minorities to surmount. This history has helped to generate and perpetuate a number of gross misconceptions.

18

MISCONCEPTION #1:

Golf is for rich, white men

Many women and minorities shy away from the game because they believe one or several of the misconceptions that continue to surround the game. Some of this misinformation is rooted in the history of the game. Like most sports, from its origin to fairly recent times, golf was the purview of men, specifically white men. But over the last three decades or so, this custom has been eroding. Not only has the game opened up on the national/international level—consider Althea Gibson, Tiger Woods, Annika Sörenstam, Laura Ochoa, Cheyenne Woods—it has become an activity that women and men in most communities, schools, and churches enjoy.

Though discrimination of women and minorities still exists, the opportunities and benefits of playing golf far outweigh the restrictive practices from the past. Women and minorities are the fastest growing population playing the game of golf. On any given day, you can walk onto a golf course and play in a foursome with anyone from anywhere in the world, of any gender, of any ethnicity, and from any walk of life. Everyone is playing golf now.

MISCONCEPTION #2:

A related misconception is that golf is a game for the rich. It's just too expensive!

When people make this statement I always answer, "Compared to what?" Think about the cost of tickets to any major sporting event, taking clients out for lunch or dinner with drinks, buying that fabulous leather handbag and matching shoes,

19

or even spending a day in the spa! These are all pricey but you do them anyway, right? Right!

There's nothing wrong with that sports ticket; or the restaurant, or the spa, or the good-looking accessories.

If you want to become a competent player and benefit from the advanced networking capabilities that the game generates, you can't make excuses designed to keep you from acquiring those benefits. DON'T BE INTIMIDATED!!! Public and private clubs are competing for your business! They WANT to see you walk through that door and inquire about costs, schedules, and lessons with their certified professionals!

There are many golf courses and country clubs that offer a variety of affordable packages that will fit most budgets. Many country clubs offer a variety of packages from the most reasonable to the most expensive and everything in between. For example, Innisbrook and the Nemacolin Woodland Resorts offer corporate membership (for your business), young professional membership, and individual and family membership.

When you consider the return on your investment, if used effectively, golf as a business tool is a comparable expense and well worth every bit you invest.

MISCONCEPTION #3:
Golf takes too long to play; it's boring

Another reason people deny themselves the pleasure of learning how to play golf is not a reason at all, but an excuse for not getting out on the course. The game really doesn't take as much time as you might think. Many people say golf is boring; they are on the course, but their head is not in the game. You'll be surprised to find how fast time flies out on the course, because you are relaxed and enjoying the game.

Look at the traditional way many people conduct business: The 3-hour power lunch or a 3.5-hour dinner. You will take the same amount of time—2.5 hours/9-hour lunch or 4 hours/18-hour dinner—but the difference is, on the golf course, there are no waiters to interrupt, no friends/colleagues that may visit your table, in other words, there are no interruptions. You have a captive audience, their undivided attention, and people who know why they are playing—they are in it for the business and relationship building, business for themselves and business for you and your company. And the added advantage is the competition! Yes, the competition. Once you get involved in the game on the course and begin to control your shots, you will become excited about what your next shot will be. Golf offers the challenge of a sport, and the excitement of closing the upcoming business deal. That's why more and more professional athletes in other sports play golf!

Again, having the ability to play golf gives you a competitive edge and leverage in a concept of advanced business networking which can be used to create a successful atmosphere for building relationships that ultimately lead to doing business: a new reality.

21

CHAPTER 2

☙THE GAME

Understanding the Basics

> If you watch
> a game, it's fun.
> If you play at it,
> it's recreation.
> If you work at it,
> it's golf."
> —BOB HOPE

I n my wonderful and rewarding career as a sports manager, corporate leadership coach and adjunct professor at business schools, I've worked with many heads-of-state, diplomats, celebrities, blue chip corporate executives, MBA candidates, and lawyers in my *The Art of the Deal: Golf–Access to Success* workshop/seminars.

The two questions I'm asked most often are, "Why do I need to learn how to play golf?" and, "Why do I need it in my professional portfolio?"

The simple answer is that golf parallels life and golf parallel business. Golf is a sport intentionally designed to challenge the player to advance, to make choices, to take action, to accept the consequences of those actions and to still advance to achieve a goal. In this book, we will show you why you need the game in your portfolio and in your life. Let's take a look at the basics of the game so we can see how the game applies to life and business.

The goal of golf is to get the ball into the hole with the least number of strokes or shots. The ultimate purpose of golf as a sport is for the player to achieve such self-control that the player efficiently (with the smallest margin of error) and effectively (achieving short term targets for long term benefits) navigates the course successfully with the lowest possible score.

The game is played on many acres of landscape called the course. A regulation course consists of 18 holes, which are numbered and played sequentially. Normally, par for 18 holes is 71 or 72,

23

A MODERN HOLE

GREEN

ROUGH →

← TREES

FAIRWAY →

WATER HAZARD

BUNKER/ SAND TRAP

TREES

FORWARD TEE →

TEE BOX

Alice Dye, The first lady of golf course architecture in the United States was credited for bringing forward tees to the game and for "improving enjoyment in golf for the average or beginning player."

depending on the course yardage. Usually, the first half or the course is called the front nine and the second half, the back nine. The challenge along the course is increased by the landscaped configuration of the course design.

To remove any confusion, the term "hole" has two distinct meanings. Each of the 18 parts of the course is a hole, for example the first hole or the seventh hole. Each of these holes has a starting point, the tee or tee box, and an ending point, called the hole or the green.

Each of the numbered holes has a very different landscaped configuration and length/ distance designed to challenge players' abilities. A player starts at the tee and hits the ball out across a broad, evenly cut, grassy area, called the fairway, which extends down the middle of the numbered hole leading to the finely cut, carpet-like area surrounding the hole/cup, which is called the green.

Golf courses are designed with a terrain to challenge players which is why each hole requires different shots and techniques. There are fourteen clubs in a regulation set in your golf bag.

24

Each club is designed for different types of shots. Each shot, from the tee, fairway, rough or traps requires focused concentration before and during execution.

Another level of intentionally designed challenge is found on the green itself. The green is comprised of extra fine grass, closely cut to create what appears to be a smooth carpet. Don't be fooled. The green can be as subtly deceptive as a mine field. A player must cultivate a sense of knowing how to read the green. You may have observed professional players competing in tournaments get down on their knees to take a lower visual profile of the green. This low-angle point-of-view allows them to see undulations in the area they're playing that lead to the cup/hole.

To reiterate the basics of the game, playing golf is a test of a player's skill and ability to play at or below par, by getting the ball onto the green and into the cup/hole with the least amount of shots or strokes.

So, the course is intentionally designed to parallel life. The game itself is challenging: hitting a little ball out into a vast area of unknown territories. Having the self- control to make the ball go where you want it to go, at the speed and distance that you want it to travel, with the accuracy you have envisioned, like life and business requires, stamina, patience, technique, determination, stick-to-itiveness, and a sense of humor. Golf is parallel to life and business.

25

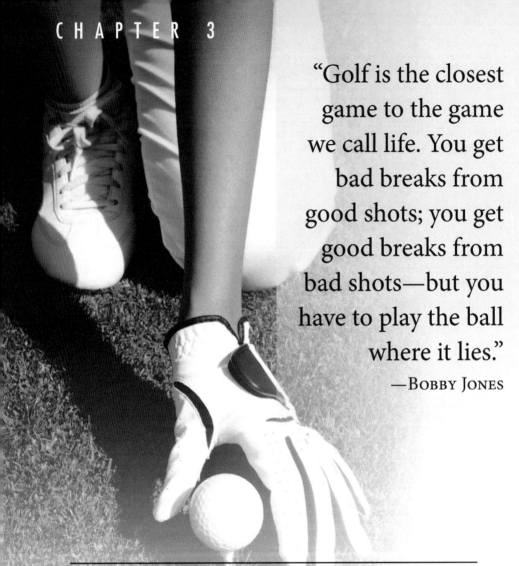

"Golf is the closest game to the game we call life. You get bad breaks from good shots; you get good breaks from bad shots—but you have to play the ball where it lies."

—BOBBY JONES

⁓GAME THEORY & PRACTICE

Why golf works

The critic in you might say "Whatever you get out of golf, you can get out of other sports or other social endeavors." I say, "While each sport has its benefits, its own attractive features, none match golf for its application to developing business." Here are 18 reasons why.

26

1. Golf provides access and time to create an all-important goal: BUILDING RELATIONSHIPS. This is what makes golf stand out from all else as a tool for developing business.

2. Golf mirrors life and business. The opportunities and obstacles you face in both are always changing. Unlike regulation standard, or consistent fields of play, the golf course is different from the tee through the fairway, from roughs and hazards to the green and the cup. Golf mirrors life and business.

3. Golf is a wonderful tool for self-development. Through practice it elevates your self-confidence and empowers you to achieve more success by increasing your passion for perfecting your skills and your game.

4. Golf is a fine measuring stick to reveal the qualities, or lack thereof, of a person's character; you get to know yourself and it gives you deep insights into others; you get to assess characters and personality types, and to value honesty and fair play. All of these traits and characteristics, of course, are transferrable from the golf course to the conference/office boardroom. In the domain of business, especially on the executive level, golf has increasingly become a new screening tool.

5. Golf levels the playing field. Women and men can play the game together and the playing field is level. CEOs and their staff can play together and the playing field is level. Golf transcends race, gender, wealth-status, age, and religious beliefs. Golf is an effective tool for breaking down barriers and creating new clients, and new relationships. If you have an opportunity to get on the golf course with your boss or other superiors, you are now on the level playing field: all are there for the same purpose, to play the game of golf.

27

6.   Golf provides the opportunity to become a more conscious and mindful communicator in business interactions where you must know what and what not to do, and when and when not to speak.

7.   Golf is not a contact sport; it is a sport that's all about making contacts! Golf provides an unparalleled setting for networking. Through building relationships you become part of networks that can enhance business. Players in groups of two, three or four go out on the course and match their skills and abilities, have a great time doing it, engage in great conversations, and have fun competing for the best scores as individuals and as a group. It promotes positive competitive camaraderie.

8.   One might think if you get degrees and work hard you can achieve your goals. Although these assets are unquestionably important, they do not prepare you to meet the boss or to communicate effectively with her/him once you do. Golf gives you the opportunity to interact with superiors and the time to develop long-lasting lines of communication.

9.   Golf has in-built honor codes and systems of self-governance because players keep their own scores, call penalties on themselves, and sign off to verify that their scores are accurate and true.

10.   Golf has an in-built sense of equity and fairness in scoring because the handicap system allows player's with differing degrees of proficiency to compete against each other on somewhat equal terms.

11.   Golf, like the game of chess, helps to systemically challenge you to visualize and to think two, three, four moves ahead.

12.   Golf helps you to stay healthy, and you can play it for a lifetime. It keeps you fit and reduces stress. It provides you with a mentally and physically healthful day of reasonable exercise, out in the open air. It promotes a dynamic atmosphere of positive energy, and allows people to relax, and get into themselves.

13.   Golf provides you an extraordinary ROI–Return On Investment– of your time, effort, and expenditures.

14.   Golf is unique in its playing field; no two courses are alike. Unlike other sports – for, example basketball and tennis courts and baseball, football, and soccer fields are always the same regulation sizes. In each of these games the players know that the parameters are constant. But in golf, the terrain is unpredictable. So golf, like business, has many different contours and challenges. Each hole requires different shots and strategic techniques where you must concentrate and focus on each shot before execution.

15.   Golf promotes boardroom diversity and strengthens existing business relationships. From a business professional point of view, understanding the game, and being able to play it, attracts new business partners.

16.   Golf expands your worldview, gives you a global mindset, even if you already possess one. It enhances that by building your perspectives and appreciation for the cross-cultural interactions of diversity. This is also significant as golf has standard rules observed around the world.

17.   Golf is an effective platform for corporate public relations and fundraising to support charities and worthy public causes by generating money, awareness, and branding for them. Another

29

important aspect, in the overview of business development, is that the sponsoring agencies also rely on the participation and goodwill of business and government leaders, celebrities, professional athletes, and the public to support the causes.

18.   Golf is that magic tool that helps you break through the glass ceiling. I strongly encourage you to invest in some equipment; hire the services of a professional to teach you the basics; join a public, private, or semi-private club; get out on the course; and improve your standing - in the professional and business world. Golf provides social interaction, which follows after the game is wrapped up. This setting, when the moment is right (see A.J. Bell-Reed's Praise for *The Art of the Deal–Golf: Access to Success* in the praise section), allows for another level of the game: turning the bonding and relationship building energy earned out on the course into business interactions.

"A male founding partner in one of my firms was very successful, and his counsel was highly sought in a specialized practice. I was very often asked what I considered to be the reason for his success….to the surprise of the inquirers, my answer was always the same: 'He learned to golf.'"

—Susan, 60-Something,
Best Friends at the Bar
by Susan Smith Blakely

At this point, I'd like to share six stories from my own playbook. As you read through them you can see these eighteen reasons in play in response to **why golf works**.

Peter Matseke, M.D. — South Africa

A successful physician and healthcare executive in South Africa, Dr. Peter Matseke, wears a coat of many colors, and one of those coats reflects the style of an avid golf enthusiast.

But that wasn't always the case. When Peter Matseke developed an interest in golf in the 1990's, a very small number of black people were playing golf in South Africa. The game, of course, can be quite expensive. However, with the advent of golf superstars like Tiger Woods, more South Africans, especially young people, have developed an interest for the game. In fact, some private schools in South Africa now offer golf as a sport.

In 1982, Peter completed studies to become a physician and he worked hard to establish a successful family medicine practice in Soweto.

He got down in the trenches with compassionate and extensive hands-on care, helping people who really needed the kind of quality medical attention he could provide.

These experiences include the development of a hospital, commissioned healthcare services, special project management and staff training, all of which presented Peter with a wide range of opportunities that also sparked an entrepreneur's eye for business – and social transformation.

Today, Peter is the founding CEO, managing director and primary shareholder of the Clinix Health Group, a rapidly developing network of health services clinics in an organization offering a wide array of disciplines, including radiology, pathology, obstetrics, gynecology, orthopedics, pediatrics, general medicine, pediatrics and adult intensive care,

31

otolaryngology, ophthalmology, urology, psychiatry, maxilla facial surgery, dentistry, physiotherapy, and pharmacy control and management.

Peter is quite adept at identifying and initiating business opportunities in his home country of South Africa, across the African Continent, and in the international business community.

One element of Peter's success is his keen ability to identify business opportunities that are right in line with his ongoing commitment as a healthcare provider, and he enjoys a well-deserved reputation as a visionary entrepreneur, accumulating a sensational track record for profit generation and return on investment.

Peter's enthusiasm about the game of golf evolved over time and is characterized by a certain belief that golf is an instrument for natural selection regarding people he wants to do business with.

"Golf is a great test for honesty"

"I have found that when you play golf you are able to make assessments of the character types and value systems of the people you are playing with. Golf is a great test for honesty," Peter says. "I've played with some people who want to win at any and all costs – and who aren't beyond going to extremes to do so..."

Early on, however, whenever any conversation between us turned to golf, Peter subscribed to the notion that, "Golf is not a game for manly men," and would assert that the only sport worth watching or participating in was football. "Not the American brand, but the real football." By which, of course, he meant the game we in the States call soccer.

As things sometimes have a way of happening, especially in the lives of highly successful people, Peter found himself at the beginning stages of an important business relationship with the CEO of a firm in Germany who asked Peter if he could play golf?

Shortly thereafter, I received an international telephone call from Peter, asking me to select a set of golf clubs and outfit him in every way he'd need to get out on the golf course with his new client.

Today, Peter smiles as he remembers his first game of golf twelve years ago.

"It was at Selbourne Country Club and my USA-based friend Rose Harper sent me a brand new set of clubs. I asked my caddie which club I should use to hit the ball, at which point everyone within earshot burst out laughing. From that day on, I was determined to master the game." Peter came to golf as a cynic but today he's an enthusiastic player who gets out on the course whenever he can, including playing rounds with his son, Kgolo.

"The Clinix Health Group has hosted or sponsored numerous golf games to fundraise and promote worthy causes. We recently held a Golf Day at South Africa's popular Zimbali Lodge golf estate for the 60th anniversary of the medical school at University of KwaZulu-Natal, my alma mater. We've also sponsored tourneys for churches, schools, and the South African National Forces."

> "I now see the golf course as an extension of the boardroom, the new boardroom"

Today, whenever Peter is asked for advice about how a rookie should approach learning and playing the game of golf, he states that in the initial stages one would need coaching and enthusiastic people to play with.

"The beauty of golf is that you can play for as long as you are healthy. The game is very relaxing and quite valuable as a networking tool in business ventures in that it informally helps you assess the type of person you are playing with and whether you would do business with them. I now see the golf course as an extension of the boardroom, the new boardroom," Peter concludes.

Here now, in the year 2014, Peter is adding a Master's Degree in Sports Science to his already impressive credentials. He also has a pretty good golf handicap. ■

33

Kathryn Crosby — The Crosby Connection

I first met Kathryn Crosby through our mutual friend Dolores Hope, wife of Hollywood great and another avid golfer, the late Bob Hope. While writing this book, Kathryn was one of the first people I asked to share memories about our first meeting, the kinship that followed, and to recall her own love affair with golf.

"Rose and Dolores Hope were very close, great friends," Kathryn recalled. "Dolores was an angel and a spectacular lady golfer who often came back east to support the Crosby Invitational at Pebble Beach. She could even beat her husband – and Bing's great friend – Bob Hope, which Bob hated, but was a very good sport about it. It was Dolores who suggested that I recruit Rose to support my work with the Crosby Invitational, and when I met her I was very impressed. She had an impeccable knowledge of golf and sports management. I recognized Rose as a real problem solver and I asked her to serve on the board of the Crosby Invitational. That was a great decision because she made valuable contributions. My old friend Walter Annenberg told me: 'What you want in a board member is for them to give, get, or get off!' Rose has definitely been a go-getter for the Crosby. She's a savvy advisor and has been very flexible with her time, which is a big plus in a board member!"

Kathryn fully agrees that careers can be made on the golf course, and women have progressively learned that playing the game is as important a contributor to getting ahead in business as making good presentations in the board room. "Rose has helped many women build their careers by introducing them to golf and through her Grass Ceiling Workshops. You can learn so much about people on the golf course, assess their code of honor and whether they will keep their word in business and respect you as a woman. Her Grass Ceiling presented *"The Art of the Deal: Golf–Access to Success"* workshop/seminars actually shatter the grass ceiling, which is the idea that women aren't welcome on the golf course", Kathryn continued. "Actually, from what I've seen, men love playing golf with women who are sociable, diplomatic and can play, even just a little. And it's

Left to right: H.E. Edith Grace Ssempala, Ambassador of Uganda to the US; H.E. Sheila Sisulu, Ambassador of South Africa to the US; Gloria Redman, President & CEO of Triumph Technologies Inc., Alexandria, VA, USA; H.E. Ivonne A-Baki, Ambassador of Ecuador to the US; along with me and Kathryn Crosby.

35

afterwards, when you're having drinks in the club house that you focus on doing business. Which is why in her *"The Art of the Deal: Golf–Access to Success"* workshop/seminars, Rose puts very high emphasis on women taking golf lessons and sharpening their sense of when it's right to talk business."

Kathryn has also been a big supporter of mine and events that I produced. She's played in my tournaments and during one of those tournaments she had the pleasure of meeting and playing with basketball great Michael Jordan! She also served as the keynote speaker at a workshop/luncheon I presented in Washington, DC.

"I was honored to speak at a stellar event Rose had for lady diplomats in Washington that was hosted by the then-ambassador of South Africa to the United States, Sheila Sisulu. The event included fourteen female diplomats and several DC-based media celebrities, all of whom took part in the Art of the Deal: Golf workshop/luncheon followed by some time on the practice area. Some of the participants even went on to play a full nine holes.

It was a wonderful networking event and local TV stations even came out to cover it. They were an important group of ladies and very good sports, and we all had a marvelous time…" ■

William "Bill" Caldwell — The Crosby Invitational

Rose Harper and long-time golf partner William "Bill" Caldwell, Senior Vice-President of the Sarah Lee Company at the Bing Crosby Invitational Golf Tournament.

When I first began participating as a player in the Bing Crosby Invitational Golf Tournament, an annual charity tourney in which I take part in to this day, I was listed as what is called one of the "designated celebrity players." The designated players were amateur golfers at this renowned annual event, held in Winston-Salem, North Carolina, who were like pinch-hitters in baseball. The requirement of four days of competition at "The Crosby" – was not possible for some corporate and celebrity players, and so the designated players were called on to fill in the foursome until their player arrived.

This allowed celebrity players like me, who could be there a full week, to fill in the vacancies by playing as a member of various corporate teams in the competition. I would fill the vacant spot until the corporate players or others arrived, which usually meant that I was playing with a different corporate team each day of the event. This, of course, offered me tremendous networking opportunities and I enjoyed meeting new team members each day.

On the opening day of play, I would sometimes tee off to officially open the event along with the host, my friend Kathryn Crosby.

As the tournament got underway, each day I would check in with the Pro Shop to see who I had been paired with. One day about my third year as a designated player, I was paired with William "Bill" Caldwell, a corporate executive. Also playing in our group was a very high-profile NFL coach (who shall remain nameless), and his partner in play. It became obvious from the first tee that the football coach and his partner had never been teamed with a female golfer, and they made their discomfort visible by questioning whether I had my putter and by making other subtle, and not so subtle, disparaging comments. I was playing from the forward tees. So after the three men teed off behind me, my partner Bill and I proceeded forward to my tee, but the coach and his partner started moving out and across the fairway. Bill called out, warning that I had to hit, but they ignored him and only moved over along the side of the fairway. On the second hole, they repeated this same testosterone-driven performance, and Bill was upset and pretty fed up with the way these men were disrespecting his partner. We all tied the scores on the first and second holes. On the third hole they continued their antic of moving down the fairway in front of me before I took my shot. Bill was about to call them back again, but I asked him not to waste his breath, "Let's just play our game," I said.

We were on the tee at a long par five with a lake set right center of the fairway and out-of-bounds was close to the left side of the fairway. Having played this course many times in previous tournaments, I knew exactly how far my drive would go, and that there would be no danger whatsoever of my drive going anywhere near the lake. Meanwhile, as the coach and his partner were making their way down along the right side of the fairway, I hit a career high tee shot that sailed over their heads and stopped about two feet short of the lake! Bill and I laughed hilariously, high-fived each other and went on to Birdie and win the hole. From that point on, we never let up on them, winning our 18-hole match quite handily!!!

After the game, Bill said, "That was great fun, Rose! I'd like to team up with you again tomorrow!" I told him I would love to join him again and that I really enjoyed my time playing with him and having him as a partner, with the caveat that I was still a designated player and not assigned. I explained that I was a corporate fill-in, and he'd have to "know somebody" to make a special request for us to team up two days in a row. All he said was "Oh, okay. Look, I'll see you inside for lunch and drinks…"

> "Well, yesterday you said that I needed to 'know somebody' to play with you again, not that I actually had to be somebody…"

That next morning I checked in with the Pro Shop to see who I'd been assigned to play with and lo and behold: There was my name right next to Bill Caldwell's! For an instant I thought I was looking at the same tee-sheet from the previous day's play, so I questioned the Pro about my pairing. He said, "That's correct, Ms. Harper. Mr. Caldwell requested you," and added, "Do you know who Mr. Caldwell is?" I said "No, I only know he's a great guy, a good golfer, a lot of fun, and a real gentleman. Other than that I don't know anything about him…" The Pro then went on to tell me that Bill Caldwell was the Senior Vice-President of a division of the Sarah Lee Company, which was the parent sponsor of The Crosby! Later, when I met Bill on the golf cart, I asked "Why didn't you tell me you were 'somebody'?" He laughed and said, "Well, yesterday you said that I needed to 'know somebody' to play with you again, not that I actually had to be somebody…"

Bill Caldwell and I remain friends and was a team for the next 15 years, during which time I became a member of The Crosby Tournament Board, and a Crosby Ambassador for the Bing Crosby Scholars Program, we teamed up again and again achieving great finishes, having loads of fun and winning close to $500,000 in purses which were donated to our favorite charities. That's how golf works!!!

Bill and I are good friends to this day, and I have tons of other great Bill Caldwell stories from The Crosby, but I think I'll just hold onto those for my next book, a memoir… ■

FOUR

Rose Harper — In Japan

Yeah that's me!

2ND PEGASUS INVITATIONAL CHARITY PRO-AM
NOVEMBER 6-7, 1982 KARUIZAWA 72 GOLF

When I was a player manager/agent on the PGA circuit, I organized an exhibition appearance of my clients at an all-male outing charity invitational for Mobil Oil in Japan. The golf club was located in a beautiful mountain resort area in Karuizawa. Unfortunately, one of the professional players was a no-show, resulting in one of the exhibition foursomes to be short a player. One of the American professionals mentioned to the host members of the group that "Rose is a pretty good player!"— and then the host of the event approached me and asked if I would play in the group. It was a very cold and foggy day and I really wasn't feeling into it, being unprepared without any equipment or proper clothes to play in. Very quickly, as I was on the verge of declining the invitation, they outfitted me in a small men's cashmere sweater, a rain suit, a pair of small men's shoes, and a set of clubs. Because it was so cold I also felt I could use some additional fortification, so I asked for a cup of hot Sake!

When we teed off, due to the heavy fog, we could just barely see 50 yards ahead of us on the course. After about two holes, the sun came out and burned off the fog and we continued to play a full 18 holes, with my foursome placing high at the top! Word spread in Japan about my playing with the men and doing well, and at the tourney I organized in Japan the very next year, I was fully accepted by the men, who spoke directly to me, and looked me in the eye when talking business. And also, for the first time, there was a Japanese female newspaper reporter attending the event. At the end of the next tournament, I was the only female invited to attend a post-tourney dinner with all the men at a Geisha house, a sign of respect and real groundbreaking stuff for a Black woman in Japan!

I share this story because not so many years prior (1982), few Asian women were respected or taken seriously in the professional sports industry. Now you see great female players from Japan, Korea and China making their mark on the LPGA circuit!

"Golf Works." ■

Joe Hardy — Nemacolin Woodland Resorts

The Hardys and Rose Harper at the Nemacolin Woodland Resorts for the Annual Invitational Golf and Tennis Tournament.

I met Mr. Hardy more than 20 years ago when he brought his Marketing team to Washington, D.C. to promote his golfing Resort. He had a high profile TV personality as the spokesperson for the Resort. After the presentation, I made inquires about the venue, in regards to its capability to host our major celebrity golf tournament, so he invited me to come up and take a look.

I, along with several members of my advance-crew, made the near 3-hour trip – which was a beautiful drive through the mountains of Pennsylvania. Our initial review of the venue, after a tour led by Mr. Hardy himself, was that it could not host our well-established corporate, political, celebrity golf and tennis tournament as the existing hotel was too small and there were no tennis courts. However, it was a great golf course.

Mr. Hardy, so nonchalantly, asked what we needed. I was making my case that we needed more rooms and tennis courts, as we had not only very avid golfers but a great group of celebrity tennis players, like Hank Aaron and the young Venus & Serena Williams. He said, "Okay let's take a look around, we are going to build some villas, and there will be enough rooms. Let's take a look for a good spot to build some tennis courts, how many do you need?" This was around February and our event was scheduled for August of the same year. At the time of my first site visit I had no knowledge of who Joe Hardy was, other than that he was the owner of Nemacolin Woodlands Resorts, a destination property, up in the mountains.

I tried to convince him that there was not enough time to have this place ready for us and, quite frankly, I thought he was kind of putting me on just to see how I would react to such an outlandish proposal. So I said, "That sounds great, however, if these plans were to fail, it would be quite damaging to our foundation, our reputation, and potentially the funds we raise for college students."

In my next book I will elaborate on all the interesting details of this story but, in the end, the facility was ready for us with flying colors. The inclusion of a runway to accommodate our private corporate jets coming to the event, which was a great success and a win/win for both parties, produced very positive business development and sponsorships for both of us.

We introduced our corporate sponsors, participants, and guests to Nemacolin for the first time, and many of them are still booking their events at Nemacolin for their own corporate outings at this facility. Also, Mr. Hardy was one of the first sponsors of my *"The Art of the Deal: Golf–Access to Success"* seminar/workshops for peer level corporate women. ∎

Ed Dwight — The Game of Golf:
Personal Development & Career Opportunities

I met Ed Dwight more than 30 years ago as an exhibiter at my annual celebrity golf tournament. It is a friendship that continued to blossom over the years. From his foundry in Denver, Colorado, he would ship his marvelous sculptures to the events, wherever they were held, around the country, which made a significant contribution to the foundation. He is a master sculptor and a true Renaissance Man. Here is a story from his playbook from one of our many conversations.

As a kid of the Depression, living a hard scrabble life on the outskirts of Kansas City, KS, the word 'Golf' was not in my vocabulary, as I had never heard the term and would not associate it with a sport. I knew Baseball. As a teen my family moved downtown two blocks from the only All-Black High School in the state of Kansas. I then learned there was also football, basketball, and track. I spent hours at the practice field and stadium watching other black kids revel in these popular sports. Kansas City was also a center of professional Boxing, which rivaled Black Baseball in popularity. Being very small for my age, I was constantly being teased, taunted & punched. My reaction to this victimization was to start boxing in a ring, as a method of defending myself. I retired from boxing after 5 years and became the bantamweight Gold Gloves Champion of Kansas City, KS.

At high school age, my mother decided that I was not going to attend the All Black High School two blocks from our house, but would integrate an All White Catholic High School. With my Dad, a star athlete and local sports hero, I could not wait to participate in any other organized sport I could, just to make it a part of my life. I immediately garnered a position on the high school football team, and later became quite a star on the track team because of my speed. Unlike the All Black High School, with only the sports of football, basketball, and track, the White High School also had a Baseball Team, a Tennis Team and a strange sport called Golf, a sport where you used these funny looking sticks called clubs and you didn't run, jump, or hit somebody. What a waste of a man's enormous energy – I thought, so I wiped the usefulness and concept of it out of my mind.

Fast-forward several years to my successful entry into the U.S. Air Force and becoming an Air Force Officer and Jet Pilot. Being hyperactive, I still worked out in the gym with boxing and even ran track on an Air Force team or two. As an officer, I lived in Base Officer Housing. Base Officer Housing was always situated on or around a golf course. For a long while, I watched my white fellow officers play by my home on the 8th Hole, until I couldn't take it anymore. I never saw such camaraderie, but more importantly, I watched the total breakdown of the staid, strict, military chain of command, and protocol, where Lieutenants, Captains, Majors and even Colonels played together, laughed and joked like there was little difference in their military status. Hmm!

> "What was the magic of this game of golf that leveled the playing field and refuted what we learned in Officer training that we must fear and respect our Senior Officers?"

As a Junior Officer, I was smitten by the sheer "chill and awe" of just seeing an Oak Leaf, or an Eagle insignia on the crisp uniforms of my higher ranked officer personnel. Yet I was seeing my fellow Junior Officers playing golf and joking with these upper echelon powerhouses. What the devil was going on? What was the magic of this game of golf that leveled the playing field and refuted what we learned in Officer training that we must fear and respect our Senior Officers? As my observations unfolded in front of me like a blooming flower,

45

I saw the answer as to why some of my fellow young officers were getting some better assignments and being moved to the "fast track" for promotion. As I moved from base to base, I put these golfing facts into my "gee whiz" file and waited for the right opportunity to see if this golf thing really worked.

I knew nothing of playing golf, but I am a quick study. The good news is that officers did not need to purchase golf clubs, all one had to do was go to the Clubhouse and check out a set of clubs for free. I did not feel competent to ask to join a foursome, or ask anyone else to "play a round," for fear of making an ass out of myself. But needless to say, every evening right before sunset, I would start a round and play until it got dark. I would imitate the drives, strokes, and mannerisms I saw and I finally made my move at playing with the "big guns" and Walla! In nothing flat I did in fact become "one of the boys." I got promoted to Captain a year early and was placed on "fast track" for promotion. I was naturally a very hard worker, but was given all kinds of plum jobs and was given all manner of awards for just doing my job. I was appointed to the position of the only Air Force Officer to serve on the Civilian San Francisco Air Traffic Control Board and went to just about every career improvement course available. It was also from this position that I became the First African American to be selected for Astronaut Training. ■

> "Success is where preparation and opportunity meet."
> —Bobby Unser

Now you can see *Why Golf Works!*

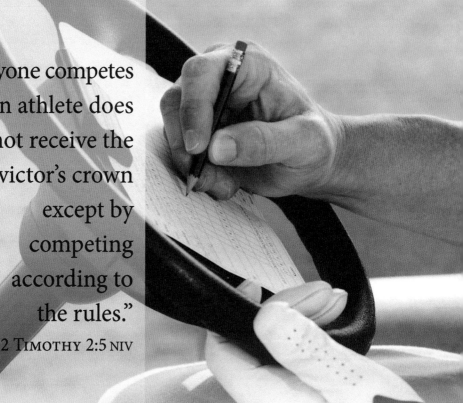

CHAPTER 4

> "...anyone competes as an athlete does not receive the victor's crown except by competing according to the rules."
>
> —2 TIMOTHY 2:5 NIV

℘RULES AND ETIQUETTE

The importance of following the rules

"**U**nlike most sports, golf expects its rules to be respected. They are not viewed as burdensome restrictions to the conduct of the game, but rather as a framework in which a competition can proceed fairly. It must be remembered that other sports have a fixed common field with one ball in play for all to see. Golf, on the other hand, can have 150 balls in play at one time over 160 acres of unique topography. Without ease of monitoring the game, players are expected to call penalties on

48

their fellow competitors and, most importantly, on themselves. Yes, there are referees and the USGA Rules Committee; however, the participants themselves provide the first line of scorekeeping. Officials are present to simply assist the player. One of the unique features of golf is the attesting procedure in stroke play where the player, via his signature, attests to his score. *Golf is a game of honor played by honorable people."*

JERRY DUFFY
Maryland State Golf Association Rules Official
Member of the USGA Senior Amateur Committee

RULES

The rules, how important are they? Knowing the basic rules can work to your advantage and to your disadvantage if you don't know them. Playing by the rules in your corporate, club, and member guest events says a lot about you and your business partners.

No one expects you to know all the rules of golf, not even the professionals know them all, that's why you see rules officials (referees) at all of the tour events. They are there to assist the players when they are in doubt or have a question about the rules. However, the players are quite knowledgeable about the rules as a whole; it's how they make their living. An infraction of the rules can cost those players valuable strokes, which means thousands of dollars or even disqualification.

Needless to say, amateurs should become familiar with the rules and know the basics of the game. Many of my clients have said to me they don't have time to read the ***Rule Book*** (about 182 pages)

49

and that it's intimidating to them. In 1952, in response to this concern the USGA and the R&A (global governance bodies of the game) made a commitment to make the rules less intimidating and more accessible for the average golfer and consistent throughout the world when they issued a unified code known as the *Rules of Golf*. These rules are reviewed every two years for any revisions adopted by both parties.

The USGA has published an eight page summary card of some of the principle rules of golf and etiquette entitled *A Quick Guide to the Rules of Golf (formerly Golf Rules in Brief)*. I have found this to be an invaluable card as it addresses just about all of the basic rules. I make sure all of my clients have a copy in their golf bag. While over the years I have come across a great number of little pocket golf books explaining the USGA rules and etiquette, I find this guide to be more user-friendly.

One of the important rules most amateurs don't know and/or pay attention to is the *pace of play*. USGA Rule 6-7 states: **"The player must play without undue delay and in accordance with any pace of play guidelines that the Committee may establish."** This is a rule, not an option or choice to play at your own pace. While women for the most part are still experiencing gender bias by the *rangers* (people who monitor the pace of play) on the course, all the more reason why women should become familiar with this rule, as all rules carry a penalty just as, for example, grounding your club in a hazard carries a penalty.

More golf clubs are posting *time guides* along the course to aide players to know where they should be at a certain time on the course. This is an indication that you should know and respect this rule. Remember, you are not the only group on the course. It's a matter of respect and common courtesy for others to keep up the pace of play at all times.

One of the most common reasons for so much slow play today is that too many amateurs are playing from the wrong tee, a common practice among male players. Most courses have at least three sets of tees to choose from, other courses have up to six sets of tees. You should choose the tee according to your handicap and how far you can advance the ball.

This formula to calculate the yardage takes the ego out of the game.

Although many golfers refer to the forward tees as "ladies tees," this is a term that has been obsolete for some time. When you are playing on a new course, a knowledgeable starter can help you with the local knowledge of the course and recommend the appropriate tee. This information will set the tone for an enjoyable round of golf.

The first time I had the pleasure of playing at Rock Harbor (Winchester, VA)—a great golf course— there were five sets of tees. One of the friendliest, most knowledgeable starters not only gave us great tips for the course but had an excellent formula for selecting the correct tee. The formula he used he had read in an article in the Wall Street Journal, and you can use it too: take the

51

distance (yards) you can hit your 5 iron and multiply that by 36 and that tells you which tee to use. For example, if you hit your 5 iron 165 yards then you should use the tee closest to 5,940 yards (165 X 36 = 5,940). The tee yardage distances are located on the scorecard, for your reference. This formula takes the ego out of the game. By using the correct tee for our foursome on a new course, we completed our round in a reasonable four hours.

Another problem on golf courses today with new and seasoned players is the use of mobile phones while playing. Unless you are essential personnel, you need to shut your mobile off or put it/them on the mute mode. If you have to wait at the tee, you can always look at your calls, but to have phone conversations while playing is absolutely out of order, disruptive, and rude to your playing partners. I discourage the use of your phone, you are there to relax, bond with your partners and have fun. You would not use your cell phone in a board room/ meeting, so don't on the course.

> "The most universal quality is diversity."
> —MONTAIGNE, 1580

ETIQUETTE

One One of the most serious and common breaches of the rules is the lack of etiquette on the course. I believe this is due to the fact that most new and beginning golfers are taking golf lessons to learn the techniques of the game, how to execute the shots, but not how to manage or conduct themselves on the course. This again, is where *A Quick Guide to the Rules of Golf*, particularly the first section under General Points, becomes especially valuable. In this section, it lists the three most common details golfers should know about etiquette. These pointers are important especially in business golf, as you will be judged on your conduct or lack thereof on the course.

New golfers don't realize how much time they need to get to the course before their scheduled tee time, so as not to be late for the tee off. If you have a tee time at 8am, you should be at the course at least thirty-five minutes before tee off to change and check in

53

with the pro shop and your playing partners. If you plan to hit practice balls before teeing off, give yourself a good 45 minutes to get ready. Your tee off time means "ball in the air" at that time, not walking to the tee or just arriving. This is another form of inconsiderate, discourteous and rude treatment of your partners and the other persons who have scheduled tee times.

Another common breach on the golf course is not recognizing, respecting, and positively interacting with other nationalities, ethnicities, and cultures. Golf is a global game, played by many in today's complex international business society. Jokes, jibes, disparaging religious and political comments follow the old adage: never talk about religion or politics—they have no place on the course or in the clubhouse.

It is important that when we enter other people's cultures, we are open to receive and learn from them without imposing our own. Often times, you will see people avoid people from different cultures on the course, playing among their own kind because of the fear of the language barriers or other biases. However, more and more businesses are recognizing the value of this global diversity tool and encouraging their employees to get out on the golf course for a different personal experience.

A great book on international etiquette business, *Kiss, Bow, or Shake Hands: How to Do Business in 60 Countries* (Terri Morrison and Wayne A. Conaway) is an excellent, easy-to-read book for anyone interested in business golf. It contains examples of how to successfully conduct international business that can very easily help you understand the value of embracing different cultures on the golf course. Having been blessed to play golf in

54

many countries around the world, I discovered that there were very few language barriers on the course. We were all there for the same game, for the same results, enjoying each other and the game and every once in a while we would understand a few words (with great joy) but we always knew the right thing to say for a good shot, and had great times after the games in the clubs.

Playing by the rules is a test of an individual's character or lack thereof. For example, take counting your score correctly. I'm not talking about making a mistake on a hole where you have had a difficult time and miscounted. But if you are consistently making a miscount for 7 or 8 holes, there's a problem. If you are rolling the ball over when you should be playing it as it lies, if you are moving the ball in the rough, if you are not marking your ball properly on the putting green, if you are throwing clubs, using harsh language, being impatient when your playing partners are hitting, etc. these are the same traits you will demonstrate in the business environment.

It usually only takes one round of golf to tell the character of a person, but it may take years in the work place to detect character flaws. In today's business culture, many managers are taking people out to play golf before hiring and or making important promotions or employee decisions just to see the character of their prospective employees or associates.

Playing by the rules and understanding golf etiquette are extremely important!

55

CHAPTER 5

THE RIGHT EQUIPMENT AND DRESS

Properly sizing and fitting your clubs

Whether you are a male, female, beginning golfer, intermediate, senior or advanced player, all should have their golf clubs fitted by an authorized professional fitter.

Like fingerprints, no one's DNA is exactly the same. You may have the same height and weight as someone else, but your hand size, arm length, swing differential, and so on will have an impact on how you perform. Your golf clubs must fit your personal body type and your game.

56

The diagram highlights the ideal 'sweet spot' to hit the ball. Hitting the ball in the middle of the clubface, is the ideal point of contact because the momentum is not lost from the club head moving and vibrating.

Properly fitted clubs can make a very positive impact for you when you get out on the course, tee-off and hit the ball on what we call: "the Sweet Spot!"

Selecting and purchasing a good set of golf clubs should be considered an investment in a business tool. I strongly recommend taking a series of lessons (ten minimum) from a professional prior to making this investment in your equipment.

We can compare making the investment in your equipment to shopping for and purchasing a high-end designer outfit. It's about what you see, what you like, what meets your budget, how comfortable you feel in the outfit, what other elements appeal such as color, fabric, and finally how flattering it is to you.

I'm using this example to illustrate how important it is for you to use the same logical approach to purchasing a set of golf clubs.

57

There are so many advertisements in golf magazines attesting to the qualities of their golf clubs, their hitting power, the accuracy of the club, and why we absolutely must have that new hybrid golf club in our bag, or that hot new putter!

However, it all comes down to what fits your body type and, of course, what you are willing to invest financially. When making the initial purchase, be certain to negotiate with your salesperson to include custom fitting as part of the deal.

Now you are ready for another series of lessons with your new clubs. Some golf schools or coaches will provide the option of video analysis as part of their instructional curriculum, so you get to see exactly what you're doing right, or where you will need improvement. You can also acquire about purchasing a DVD of your lessons to take with you to study. These visuals will help you better understand and remember golf protocols and terminologies.

Then watch your handicap go down!

According to a study by noted consumer analysts at the *Sports & Leisure Research Group*, "90% of U.S. golfers may be playing with the wrong equipment!"

This research also proves and demonstrates that custom-fitting helps beginning golfers play better, and have more fun out on the course. In addition, the researchers indicate that there are no industry standards for custom-fitting and there is much confusion existing around the subject. The survey defined custom-fitting as "the process of measuring a golfer's physical attributes and applying high-tech equipment (such as a launch

58

> ## "90% of U.S. golfers may be playing with the wrong equipment!"
> —Sports & Leisure Research Group

monitor), to capture important information on swing speed, ball flight and spin rates – all of the above designed to build the right custom – fit golf clubs for each golfer."

Some highlights of the research survey's findings show that:

- 92% of those golfers who were custom-fitted for their new equipment on a launch monitor saw immediate benefits with their new equipment.

- 80% of custom-fitted golfers hit the ball more accurately and consistently.

When I first started playing golf you just about knew the names of all golf club manufacturers, and they were very comparable, but buying new equipment today has become more complicated because of how golfers consume media and the many options available. As a beginning golfer, I did what many beginning golfers do today, I bought what I saw all the good golfers using, including the types of golf balls, even the golf apparel. However, one thing that I did do right was to take a series of lessons before I purchased my equipment. Having had lessons from a professional teacher for several months, I took to and loved the game right away, kept up with my lessons, and played every day, which caused my handicap to come down to the single digits! During those months I had

59

learned enough about the game and the mechanics of my own swing to make an educated choice for selecting my clubs.

My sister and I often play together and we have identical sets of golf clubs. However, we are not the same height or size, as I am about 5'3" and she is about 5'5", a big factor in club fitting. I was referred, by the manufacturer of my clubs, to a certified golf club fitter in my area, and we went together for fitting.

The facility had all the necessary fitting equipment to assist us, the fitter, unfortunately, didn't do a very good job.

In fact, he recorded almost identical fittings on the specifications sheet for our separate fittings. He had my clubs set 4 degrees off, which made a tremendous detrimental difference in the execution of my shots.

In 2011, I went to New York for a professional fitting and was featured in an article in *Golf Magazine*. My session was with Eric Bianchini, one of the best professional fitters in the business. It was an excellent experience. Having my clubs properly fitted by Eric made a great difference in my game and gave me more confidence about executing my shots.

• •
FITTER: Eric Bianchini

ROSE HARPER
Occupation: Management Consultant, CEO of The Grass Ceiling
Residence: Washington, DC

"Rose has a very good swing, but she tends to leave the clubface open at impact. Having an open face creates a little more backspin and decreases efficiency (i.e., transfer of energy to the ball). She needs to get the face to close more through impact,

60

which will increase ball speed and efficiency. Her current clubs are 2 degrees flat, which compounds her problem. When the lie angle is too flat, the toe catches the ground first and the heel swings open. A more upright club should make it easier for her to hit the ball from right to left."

6-IRON	OLD	NEW
Head Speed (mph)	59.6	**62.7**
Ball Speed (mph)	74.7	**82.9**
Launch Angle (degrees)	22.7	**18.7**
Backspin (rph)	5,120	**3,016**
Sidespin (rph)	614 right	**557** left
Apex (feet)	40	**37**
Dispersion (yards)	9 right	**13** left
Carry Distance (yards)	87	**100**
Total Distance (yards)	99	**121**

*Old club data taken with a 7-iron (no 6-iron in set). New club data taken with a 6-iron.

RESULT: Rose is able to square the clubface and move the ball from right to left. Shots fly, on average, 13 yards left (compared with 9 yards right). She gets more roll and increases total distance. Her ball speed jumps significantly (+8.2 mph), which gets her efficiency rating from 84 to 88 percent. (According to Bianchini, the highest efficiency rating for an iron hit in the center of the clubface, with a square face, is 94 percent.)

• •

The main thing I learned was how important it is to be properly fitted and the positive impact fitting has on your game. Eric took the time to explain all the technical information, what needed to be changed, and why. A proper fitting can empower any golfer to reach a new level of play.

61

SARAH BETH FAISON • SWEET TRADE PHOTOGRAPHY

Diversity and style on the tee.

THE ELEMENTS OF STYLE

Dress codes for the golf course have changed dramatically over the years, so much so that the *Wall Street Journal* recently dedicated three full pages to the subject, going back in time to examine close to 100 years of golf course fashions. However, a glaring omission in the article was that despite the burgeoning explosion of one of the fastest-growing markets in amateur and professional sports, there wasn't a single female outfit mentioned or displayed.

With the proliferation of redesigned, upgraded public courses, we're seeing a new generation of women golfers' on the greens, and their sense of sartorial splendor merges modern styles with classic looks which never go out of fashion. These players want to look as good as the re-styled and improved courses they're playing on, or the elegant club houses where they enjoy drinks

62

and do meetings. Yet, some decry this turn toward haute couture on and off the course as "people looking like fashion ads in magazines or billboards…"

Nevertheless, fashion statements on the courses have become a billion dollar enterprise for sportswear manufacturers who are spending millions in advertising and endorsements to keep that market growing. Writing in *Forbes Magazine* on the subject of fashion in the sports world, with special reference to professional golf, James Bartlett stated: "It's not so much what you wear on the pro golf tour, as it is about how much you get paid to wear it…"

This apparent phenomenon, this convergence of golf and fashion isn't as new as people today tend to think. Style has always had a major role in the professional domain, when some of the greats of the game like Stewart Payne, Tommy Bolt, and Doug Saunders presented themselves on the course with very distinctive looks, including knickers, hats, caps and sweater vests over shirts and ties.

However, golf fashion entered a whole realm of social and commercial impact when athletic wear manufacturer Nike agreed to do a major endorsement contract deal with the inestimable Tiger Woods for a whopping $40 million USD, to have him serve as their cover man for clothes and shoes bearing Nike's iconic "swoosh" trademark.

All of the current roster of golf magazines boast sections and four-color ads touting the latest look in fashions for the fairway, and like the men on the PGA Tour, women on the LGPA Tour have been creating their own personal image brand.

With the average age for women on the LPGA ranging from 18-36, many of the outfits they wear on the course, including

63

mini-skirts, would be an inappropriate style to wear when you, as a professional woman, are out on the course playing for the purpose of business-development networking. Apparel manufacturers compensate professional players for sporting such trendy, but unprofessional, fashions.

I am not suggesting that you have to leave your personalities in the closet. Dress to feel comfortable while still being strategic about the message you are sending. Clothes, just as the way you speak, make a statement. Young women all over the world are excited and happy about the way Michelle Obama, who did not conform to her predecessor's dress codes of suits and dresses with sleeves. She, however, dresses elegantly according to her personality and her role as first lady of the United States of America.

Yet, more and more, we see today's young executive woman mimicking the style of dress and sports fashion of those young women on the LPGA Tour, forgetting that these professional players are also, essentially "entertainers" like many, many others in the modern world of big money products and sports-related endorsements.

Truth is, it's all part of their 'day job'!

Author Allison Luris tells us in her book *The Language of Clothes* that the clothes we choose, either in a boutique or high-end store, define us and describe us—at a distance. The vocabulary of our wardrobe conveys much more to an observer or interested party then we imagine. Our sense of style informs others of our sexual identification, our age-range, the level of class, and so forth, all before any verbal exchange. To someone in a

> ## "You're on the fairway, not the runway!"
> —ROSE HARPER

business environment, especially a decision-maker, this personal presentation gives me important information (or, heaven forbid: *misinformation!*), about you.

However, answering the call from the new upward thinking female executives, there's a major trend from the runways moving onto the fairways to meet the need of the younger professionals and their styles, more cameo looks, engineered strips and graphic designs, bright colored belts, caps and gloves.

Fashion designers are very aware of new looks coming off the drawing board and from the cutting room for the corporate executive woman. Corporate women must invest in the proper course wear, which should reflect her sense of style in the corporate domain. Ideally, these women will have a fashion sense

65

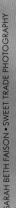

in both environments which allow her to make seamless transitions from the board room to the back nine to the club house restaurant.

The point is, your fashion style says a lot about you. Some of the things your style says about you may not be easily put into words, but they do register on the subconscious level, which means, for better or worse, an impression is made about you, who you are, and how you may or may not fit into a bigger picture or my organization. The bottom line is this: A corporate woman needs to have clothes, whether formal or casual that fit her professional lifestyle. This is an especially relevant point when you are out on the golf course with professional colleagues or with a potential or signed client.

The mantra to remember is: "You're on the fairway, not the runway!"

JEWELRY

Accessories like jewelry aren't necessarily a no-no on the course, per se, however, certain types of jewelry are definitely to be left on your dresser, in a locker at the clubhouse, or protected in your golf bag. That means: no clinky-clunky bracelets, no dangling earrings, expensive rings, pins, necklaces and especially pieces that move when you move or which catch and highly reflect the glare of sunlight. These types of jewelry items are not only inappropriate for the golf course, but can be a distraction to your playing partners.

66

SARAH BETH FAISON • SWEET TRADE PHOTOGRAPHY

Nice jewelry and cell phones, but they are inappropriate for the golf course.

Securing valuables, such as jewelry, is very important if you have a locker in the clubhouse changing room. Make sure to secure your valuables while you're out on the course. Have your caddy hold onto your valuables until you complete your rounds or put them in your golf bag. Just make sure your bag is always within your range of sight while you're out on the course, and don't forget to remove them after the game. Golf courses are generally very peaceful and secure places, but things happen.

Okay, having said all that, I like and do wear certain types of jewelry on the course for all the many years I've been a player and coach. Those pieces, however, are purposely understated.

Personal style is important, and a proper display or presentation of personal style on the golf course does not mean you negate the ability to express your individuality.

One of my mantras regarding fashion sense is this: When in doubt, seek a higher authority.

67

Boone & Sons Jewelers, located in the Washington, D.C., metropolitan area have been my jewelers of choice for more than 40 years, and over these years proprietor David Boone, also a golfer, has taught me much about why you should or should not wear certain types of jewelry on the golf course.

For example, David advises against wearing rings of any kind, especially those made of gold. Gold is a soft metal and gold rings can very easily be scratched, bent or deformed as a result of constant play and the impact of the golf club grip against the surface of the ring.

If the ring happens to have precious gemstones attached, the same issue applies, but more critically so, as sustained impacts of the club hitting the golf ball will loosen the ring's gemstones over time. Many diamonds, emeralds and other precious stones have been dislodged and lost on golf courses around the world, lost forever, for it is next to impossible to locate a lost stone on acres and acres of a fairway, even in the controlled tee-off area.

When it comes to watches, David says not all timepieces are built to withstand the constant impact of swinging and hitting the ball. Personally, I've been wearing and playing with the very same watch, the kind also worn by many professional golfers, for more than 30 years, however, it is a watch designed to withstand the kind of impact action and wear and tear that comes when one is out on the golf course.

When it comes to earrings, large hoop earrings or long dangling earrings, both of which move around a lot, they aren't appropriate for the golf course.

SHOES

Tennis shoes are NOT FOR THE GOLF COURSE! They could be very dangerous on slippery grass surfaces. I discovered these wonderful high-end stylish shoes at the PGA Merchandise Show. Perfect for the executive woman (also for men), the collection is unique. Made of beautiful supple Italian calfskin, this active footwear is designed so that it is stylish, fashionable and comfortable for on and off the course. Lacing comes in many colors to coordinate your outfits. They are also engineered for security and stability, both of which are critical to the stress of a turning body during the golf swing.

DAMEN VITELLO • HENRY & MAGDA

I am impressed that you can wear these stylish and comfortable shoes from the hotel, home, or office right to the golf course, and you are ready to tee off, and go to the club restaurant after play.

To accommodate functionality, most manufacturers are building "crossovers"—golf shoes that have utility on and off the course. When completing my advance work out on the course, which is related to a corporate client or workshop/seminars for my Grass Ceiling program, I must wear a comfortable, flexible, yet stylish, shoe.

69

Therefore, I always wear shoes that I can make my *The Art of the Deal: Golf–Access to Success* presentations in as well as make an effortless transition to play a few rounds. I've even worn some of these types of shoes when I travel by air, as they are immensely comfortable, and safe for walking on all types of surfaces.

OTHER DO'S AND DON'TS

I recall an article in *Bazaar Magazine* with the provocative title: **"How Does Power Dress?"** The answer in brief: "Powerful women don't wear ruffles and bows…"

Here then are the 'Absolute No-No's,' and the 'Okay, Maybes.'

Extra-long fingernails hamper play for obvious reasons; they make it difficult to get a good grip on the club, and in the past, there were no accommodations for golf gloves to fit the extra-lengthy nails. However, never at a loss to capture a new market, Fashion Avenue has designed gloves for women that work well for those with extra-long nails. That still doesn't apply to the actual game, however. Long to extra-long nails compromise your golf grip, and affect the proper execution of your golf shot, which isn't and won't ever be a good thing.

On the subject of protection, we ought to say a few words about the importance of proper skin care. I spoke to Dr. Cheryl

70

Burgess, a noted Board Certified Dermatologist. She offered this very important advice.

It's very important to use a good sunscreen for face, neck and arms, **regardless of your complexion**. For added protection from the sun, wear a well-fitting cap to for your head and hair, and a good pair of sunglasses for your eyes. The sun can get deceptively hot and intense on the open golf course. Sharing the results of a dermatology study performed in Australia, about the importance of taking steps to protect your skin from exposure to the sun, she said that the study revealed that "sun screen is the number one anti-aging cream in the world." This means you want to use a broad spectrum sunscreen, one that protects against Ultraviolet light; that has both A (A=Age) and B (B=Burn) class protection; that is water resistant, water proof, and sweat proof; and that has the 2014 FDA approval.

To reduce the chalkiness of some screens, she also suggests reformulating the sun screen by mixing it with a little foundation, then dusting, your face, with mineral powder, then dust with mineral powder. And you should re-apply the sunscreen after the 9th hole. She further advised that people with darker skin have a full-body exam every year by a Board Certified Dermatologist to guard against hard to detect skin cancers.

Here's a final word about the dress that is appropriate for the golf course. Everything from your clothes to how you speak makes a statement. If you want to be a woman in leadership dress the part of a powerful well-put-together woman.

CHAPTER 6

✿ HAVE FUN ON THE COURSE

Because it's not your day job!

One of the reasons I so love playing golf is that it's relaxing and
fun! Golf is not only an exquisite tool for business networking,
it's also a great and wonderful way to get a bit of exercise, and
enjoy a fun-filled day of bonding with family or colleagues!

72

I try to make a special effort to participate in all of my club's tournaments, especially the annual Ladies Member Guest Tournament, and all of the Mini-Member Guest Tournaments presented during the year. Ninety percent of the time, I extend invites to women I don't often have the opportunity to play with, including business women I want to get to know better, and female friends I know who have not played at my club previously who would like to have the experience of playing a challenging course at a fun event.

When you begin hosting guests for a round of golf be prepared, but do not become stressed. The best advice I offer to new players is: "Don't take yourself so seriously! Enjoy the game!"

Professional athletes, when they're being interviewed by sportscasters about how they are planning to play their next game (regardless of a win or loss), generally say something like: "I'm just going to get out there, do my best, have fun, and see what happens…"

Of course, professionals aren't playing the same kind of game we non-professionals engage in. We should always want to have fun and engage one another in friendly, light-hearted competition that allows everyone to have a great time. Unlike the pros, we are playing for fun, whereas with the professionals, well, that is their day job.

The truth is, only a few golfers in the world are good enough to deserve to get angry. Most likely, you are not one of them. Unless you've committed all of your time and resources to the game as a professional, you have not earned the right to act like a jerk when you happen to execute a bad shot. Furthermore, your behavior can have a negative impact on other players, and consequently negate a business deal.

73

"Don't take yourself so seriously! Enjoy the game!"

Another fun aspect of the game is the sense of accomplishment that comes when you're able to hit your shots far enough down the fairway that you get excited about advancing to your next shot! It can be quite frustrating to hit the ball and see it merely top down just 50 yards from your tee. And those feelings will be magnified if you don't know how to correct your execution. Taking lessons prior to committing to regular play with a group or partner will give you confidence and arm you with the ability to correct anything you may be doing wrong out there – so you can have fun!

Adjusting your play is an important aspect of advancing your game. For example, if you are on a par three hole, the objective is to hit the green on your first shot. However, 80% of the time the average amateur golfer misses the mark; but if you are able to get somewhere within the target zone, you get to feel good as you'll be rewarded with a chip shot on to the green, and maintain confidence in your evolving ability as you keep up with your partners.

You might not par the hole, but you are at least advancing and giving yourself a good chance to make par. So many times I have been all over the target, ending up with a bogie, a double, or worse. From my standpoint, it's not so much about what I scored on a particular hole, but if I was able to advance my shot close enough to make the next shot exciting and see me keeping up with my group.

As I've emphasized in previous chapters of *The Art of the Deal: Golf–Access to Success*, it's very important that you take a course of lessons and practice before you head out onto the golf course. Knowing what you're doing and letting your body's own physical memory kick in will guarantee that you will have fun while you're out on the fairway!

Therefore, to assure you have fun, it's an absolute must that you take a series of golf lessons before getting out on the course! Equally important is my recommendation that you take those lessons from a certified PGA/LPGA teaching professional. Find a good instructor who takes you seriously; who doesn't insist on molding you in the playing style of someone else, but who will help you develop and execute your natural style. You want a professional instructor who will ensure that you have a thorough understanding of the basics of the game, and who doesn't settle for just teaching you the game. Finally, you want an instructor who shows you how to think about the game and how to develop an internal vision that enables you to see yourself playing well— and having fun!

75

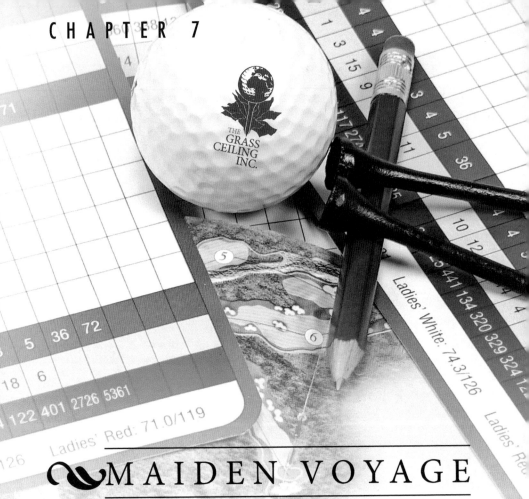

CHAPTER 7

ↄ⸿MAIDEN VOYAGE

Advance work before bringing
your first guests on the course

L ike any business venture, you should do your homework
and prepare a strategic plan. Preparing to take your
first guests out on the golf course for an outing is similar to
inviting a guest to dinner at a high-end restaurant for the
first time; you want to make the best possible impression,
make them feel welcome, comfortable and see to it that
they have a good time. To accomplish these objectives you
should have a plan of execution. There are a few things I
suggest that you do before your guests arrive.

76

MAKE SURE YOU'RE AT THE COURSE BEFORE YOUR GUESTS ARRIVE

You should take care of all of the charges (green fees and golf carts), prior to your guests arriving at the course. You want to be there well ahead of time to make sure you know where the practice range is, the restaurant and bar are located, the direction of the first tee, and that the golf clubs are on the carts in the right order. Be strategic when calling the golf course ahead of time to arrange for golf carts. It is important that you make sure your main client, and their clubs, are paired with you on your cart. By doing this you are increasing the potential of positive exchanges between yourself and the client, as a considerable amount of time is spent on the golf cart together.

Be cautious when driving a golf cart. Proper and courteous cart operation requires a lot of knowledge. These vehicles, if not operated properly and safely, can be dangerous to you and others. You should always respect the cart signs on the course. Never drive your cart close to the tee areas, putting surface, sand bunkers, or water and other hazards. It is very costly to properly maintain golf courses; therefore, if you want to continue to play a well-maintained golf course, you should do your part and respect the "No Carts Beyond This Point" signs.

77

SETTING UP THE GAME

As the host, you should always be the driver. Make sure that your clubs are placed on the driver's side (this makes the statement that you are the host.). More often than not, the male golfer will offer and sometimes insist that he drive. As an exception to the host/cart driver rule would be if you, personally, have never played the course, are unfamiliar with its layout, and one of your guests has played the course before and are more familiar, it would be

best to allow that individual to drive the cart. This also saves a lot of time by eliminating directional confusion. If you are hosting for the first time and it's a business outing, I would suggest you have a sleeve of balls, or other golf items as token gifts for your partners. I have a single golf ball packaged with my *Grass Ceiling* company logo for my guests as well as other corporate items. This is particularly helpful if you want to promote your company or business. Don't worry if they loose the balls, someone else looking for their lost ball will find it and see your company logo (A very economical way to marketing, as this further promotes your company in a very non-traditional and valuable way). As the host, its important to take the pressure off and take the egos out of the game so people can just have fun. I find it's a lot of fun to play a "best ball" twosome or a "round robin" format, where everyone in a foursome has a chance to play a little match with each other. This format is especially useful if you are not sure of the handicaps of your playing partners. You do not always have to play for individual scores.

78

DURING THE ROUND

Make sure that you keep up with the pace of play! It is very important to remember that you are not the only foursome on the course and others will be ahead or you or coming up behind. When you encounter other players, always be courteous. If necessary you should also help your partners find balls if they are having difficulty doing so; this helps to speed up play. It is the Rule, not a choice, to take only five minutes to look for your ball before you are assessed a penalty. Mark the scorecards at the next tee where you will have time while the partners are teeing off, not at the green. Also have all players in the tee box area ready to tee off and not waiting in the carts. These tactics will not only help to keep the pace of play, but will allow everyone to keep an eye on the direction of each others' tee shots.

AFTER THE GAME

Remember, you are still the host and are responsible for covering lunch and cocktails. The cool down time after a great and lively game is a good opportunity to further relax and get to know

79

Rose Harper
Chief Executive Officer

The Grass Ceiling, Inc.
P.O. Box 5874
Washington, DC 20016

THE
GRASS
CEILING
INC.

The Art of the Deal: Golf

each other better while exchanging golf stories. This is a good time for reflection and character assessments of your guest or potential client.

It's also important to bear in mind that your guests are also assessing you.

TRANSITION FROM THE GOLF COURSE TO THE BOARDROOM

Before everyone goes their separate ways, be absolutely certain that you have made the right contacts for follow-ups for a potential business deal. The lunch and cocktail setting (not on the course!!!), is the strategically correct time to exchange business cards, share and acquire information about each other's companies, etc. The exception to that rule would be that partner who cannot stay with you after the game for lunch or drinks. For this reason, you should always have a few business cards in your golf bag. The only caveat I offer is to be careful not to overkill; leave some information and details to be shared during your follow-up meetings. Try to make sure that you have positioned yourself to make that call to your partner's office and that your call will be received by your guest and that you also get the name of his/her assistant.

THANK THE GOLF COURSE STAFF

Be sure to let the club know that you appreciated their help in assisting you, and that you enjoyed their professionalism in hosting you and your guests, so they will remember you when you come again. Be aware of the staff treatment of your guests. Were they welcoming and polite to your guests? If there were things that you did not think were appropriate or found unsatisfactory, make them aware of those things as well, so they can have an opportunity to repair or fix those concerns.

REMEMBER: THIS IS NOT ROCKET SCIENCE

Relax, be in charge and have fun yourself! It's important to flow with everything and above all, not to get in your own way! None of what's been outlined here above is any different from the things you'd do in preparing any other business meeting. They are simply the normal, courteous things you would do as a good host.

81

✍ENHANCE A NON-TRADITIONAL APPROACH

Leadership Development and Diversity & Inclusion

LEADERSHIP DEVELOPMENT

Now that you've read the first 8 chapters of *The Art of the Deal: Golf–Access to Success*, it's time to examine the ways you can refine your approach to the game of golf. I'm often asked the question: "What is the difference between a **social**

golf match and a **business match?**" There are differences, and by understanding and knowing how to apply them will help build your leadership skills for developing business.

A social match is one that is usually played with family or friends; people you know well and already have easy and regular access to. These are mostly informal games set up by a simple telephone call, text message, or email to coordinate and confirm tee-times and at which venue to meet to play. No agendas involved here, just good, relaxing family/friend fun, where, as you proceed along the course waiting to get to the 19th hole, and just might meet and make some more new friends!

A business match is different altogether. The business match is designed to help you meet new people, important decision-makers in business and politics that you may not ordinarily have easy access to, and to continue relationship building with previous contacts.

83

Previously, we carefully explored the necessity for organizing and setting up your business-oriented golf matches. One of the most important things to remember in the business match is the protocol for when to Talk Business vs. Not Talking Business.

Do not bring your company's Capability Statement to the golf course. While on the course you are to concentrate on relationship building, play your best, assure the comfort-level of your guests, and play a relaxed game. Let your guest(s) take the lead. If they happen to ask you questions about your business, keep your answers short and to the point. This is the moment when you want to give that "60 second elevator speech." Keep the conversations light, so you make sure your guests are enjoying each other's company and having a great time playing along with you and one another during the game. You want to make certain to leave something to talk about after the game, using the segue way to the clubhouse restaurant or bar to capture a full-fledged, all important board room meeting, where you will then have plenty of time to present a professional overview, setting yourself up to make a more comprehensive presentation in the board room. Of course, if your guest asks for more information, do proceed to provide answers. They might be asking for more information to see what you know about your own business, how your business/product will be of value to them or whether or not they want to follow up with a meeting with you or not.

Women setting out to organize and orchestrate a business match should be just as prepared, if not more so, than any of your male colleagues. Always be ready. Keep a change of clothes in your office, and your clubs in your car or in your locker at the club. You never know when the boss might be looking for someone to play a round at the last minute with a guest, or better, you might need to invite someone at a moment's notice to play a game! I can't tell you how many times I've been called, at the last minute by a colleague, to see if I could join a group.

I was always ready, if my schedule would allow me to play. Being ready to play presented great business and social opportunities, most of which have lasted for years.

It is therefore very important for you to understand how to use this important business tool and the reasons why.

- Golf is a very valuable internal and external business incentive tool for professional growth and development.

- More women should look into taking advantage of participating in the LPGA Pro Am Tournaments, just like our male colleagues. You need to understand the value of corporate sponsorships of events and participation in golf tournaments, whether for charity or strictly corporate business-dedicated events. There are many business opportunities, benefits, and return on investment in LPGA Pro-Am participation.

85

- You need to know and understand how to select the events that work best for your corporate profile and/or programs. Don't hesitate to ask questions about the events and inquire about special opportunities that you can pay for additional exposure for your company or products.

- Women and minorities have represented the major growth factor for the game over the last 10 years, and your sponsorships should reflect the colors threaded through that tapestry. Ask the question: "Will we be able to have access to other corporate women and minorities in these events? Will women be paired comfortably with their male colleagues?"

- On the Pro Am circuit, not only will you have opportunities to play with three other corporate colleagues, but have the opportunity to be acquainted with and get to know professional golfers from around the country and the world, people who can expand your national and global network.

- Don't worry about what your handicap is! Remember: **This is not your day job.** You will learn a lot about the game from your professional golf partner, and they usually make sure they put you at ease so you can have a good time. That's their day job. Plus, they want you to come back and play next year!

- Company sponsorships of a golf event is a dynamic business promotion opportunity for your firm. More female executives need to take a good, hard look at where and how you may be spending your promotional and marketing dollars. Golf tournaments and player sponsorships make a powerful statement for your company, and you should seriously consider sponsoring female players.

A CALL TO ACTION TO MALE GOLFERS
by Mike Hoover

ATTENTION: Golf-playing male business executives – if you are looking for a great avenue to:

- Expand your network of influential decision-makers, mover & shakers
- Connect with other leaders & executives
- Develop new friendships and develop a better understanding of "how" to thrive in corporate competitive environments and boardrooms

...I am going to challenge you to consider doing something that may be as uncomfortable for you, at least at first, as it will be for the person you are asking to accept your invitation:

"Discover who they are and invite your golf playing female executive counterparts, prospects, community or industry movers and shakers to play a round of golf with you—at your club—on a weekday—partnering with some of your buds!"

Over the years I have had the joy and pleasure of many rounds of golf with existing clients, new clients, vendors, partners and strangers who turned into new clients, and up until a couple of years ago they were 100% male.

Over the past couple of years I have enjoyed several highly entertaining, well-paced and very competitive rounds of golf with several female business executives from my area. A lot of my own prejudices have been eliminated, such as:

- Women play too slow—not these women
- You can't have the same camaraderie, banter and joking around with women in the group—wrong—wrong & WRONG

87

- What about the 19th hole? What about it—they love the 19th hole as much as we do!

And I will tell you, the quality of play, the gaming and competitiveness, etc. have all been on "par" as with my male counterparts. I believe there is a genuine thirst by female executives to be invited and to participate in these opportunities. They too enjoy most of what we males enjoy about golf and they comprise a vast, vast network of business opportunities, networking opportunities and executive access that for the most part is being left un-tapped and un-accessed.

Just like I have developed life-long friendships and bonds with several of my male golfing associates over the years, I have now begun to develop these same types of relationships with female associates who I have developed an extremely high level of respect and admiration for.

To the female golfers who are saying "yes", go Mike… here is my challenge to you – STOP WAITING AROUND for an invitation and sulking if you have not yet received one!

Think about what male executives that you would like to meet, network with or further develop a relationship with and invite them to your club or course to play. Demonstrate the confidence and golf games_man_ship (Freudian slip there) that you probably want your male counterparts to witness, respect and enjoy.

One of the best years of *"Business Golf"* I ever experienced, and I kick myself every year that I fail to repeat it, was the year:

- I sat down in March and made a list of the clients, vendors, partners, etc., that I wanted to start or strengthen my relationship with

- I reviewed my calendar and blocked off an afternoon in May, June, July, August & September
- I sent an invitation (letter) to everyone on my list explaining that:
    ○ We consistently talk about "getting together,"
    ○ This is the year
    ○ Look at your calendar and let me know what day is good for you
    ○ My treat for lunch and a round of golf
    ○ Looking forward to spending some time together
- I followed through:
    ○ Anyone who did respond within two weeks I called them
    ○ They were "apologizing" to me—I had just offered free lunch and golf and they had not responded
    ○ I booked about 12 of my most important clients and partners that year—utilized key execs from my company to "fill in" when I needed a 4th and hit a home run in terms of *business development opportunities*

Why not try the same for yourself, maybe partner with another female Executive from your Club or area and co-host. I would also challenge you to establish a "game" on the first tee, demonstrate your competitive nature and ensure the round carries the spirit that most male golfers are accustomed to.

Male and female executives spending more quality time on the links is one of the most under-utilized high quality networking opportunities available to aspiring and polished executives today. – It's time to mow the "Grass Ceiling… sign up for *The Art of the Deal: Golf–Access to Success* workshop/seminars and & "Tee It Up!"

MICHAEL W. HOOVER
President
TML–A Xerox Company

89

DIVERSITY & INCLUSION

Golf is a major Diversity and Inclusion tool/vehicle of the 21st century. It is one of the most important and valuable tools for business development world-wide. For many years, corporation executives have talked about Diversity & Inclusion, but had done very little to bring this concept into true fruition.

I am pleased to see that several major corporations have taken Diversity and Inclusion more seriously, taken action, and have realized extraordinarily positive results across the board in their business profiles – and most importantly, seen measurable, positive results in their corporate bottom line.

Wherever the game is played around the planet, from Beijing to Johannesburg, from Nassau to Hawaii, golf has clearly and successfully demonstrated that it can foster diverse viewpoints that can be brought together and applied to achieving excellent results in the business world.

90

This is one of the common misconceptions about this extraordinary game. The truth of the matter is that golf transcends demographics, race, creed, religion and other arbitrary social barriers such as gender, age, economic positioning and social standing. I say that golf is the most powerful and effective diversity and leadership promoting tool in the world!

When you have the game of golf in your corporate arsenal, you will always be ready for the next big deal. Golf will help you to be taken seriously on another level of corporate and business communication, and help you to effectively grow your business in a non-traditional way. Golf has a proven track record that works for business professionals anywhere around the world.

91

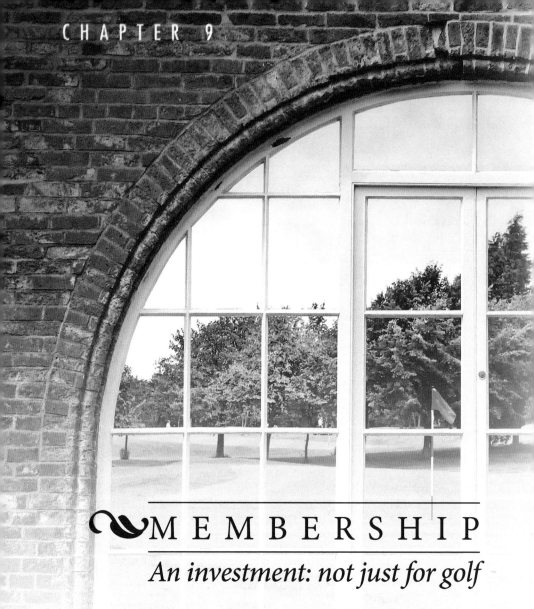

ॐMEMBERSHIP

An investment: not just for golf

Why join a club? Memberships provide access. For individuals and families; for small, mid-size, and large companies, there are many types of memberships that are affordable, that can work for you and your budget. To accommodate the emergence of the new corporate culture, the golf industry has responded by providing multiple tiered memberships and other incentive programs for young executives and emerging companies. For example, a Tournament Players Club (TPC) membership provides access to all of their network clubs, throughout the nation. Everyone does not have to join a private club to enjoy private club amenities, atmosphere, and access. Pebble Beach, Torey Pines, and Beth Page are not the only high-end public courses around the country. There are many nice ones in your area that offer very nice amenities.

SELECTING A MEMBERSHIP

When selecting a membership you should conduct due-diligence before signing up. Women owed companies should especially research and take advantage of these clubs for business development, public relations/marketing and leadership/diversity and inclusion opportunities. You should determine if the club is logistically convenient to your home or office. Does the prospective club offer the amenities you need? Clubs offer more than golf. They are also your restaurant, conference area, banquet and meeting rooms. They are places to host your company's annual holiday parties and other social events. By utilizing these amenities you will maximize the use of your membership. This could provide tax-deductible savings if you are doing business at the club.

Most large corporations own a membership at different clubs, for various reasons. Even some of the major utility companies

93

own club memberships, particularly for doing lobbying work. These memberships, however, are not made public to all of the employees, and especially women. They are usually reserved for the executive suite. I suggest that you inquire if your company owns a membership and what the criteria are for you to take advantage of using the company's club for business.

Be aware, investing in a membership is an investment in yourself and your business; therefore you should be mindful of the restrictions, if any, for women and minorities in the club's policy. For example, are there tee time restrictions for women, as well as other clauses that would not serve you well? It is important to take a look at the structure of the Board. Is it a diverse Board? Are there separate rules for men and women?

Unfortunately, still in 2014, after a five-year legal struggle, four women had to sue their club for discrimination for operating separate-sex grill rooms and by reserving prime tee times – including those coveted Saturday morning slots – for its male members. These women were paying the same initiation fees and monthly dues as the men. They won their case, possibly costing the club an estimated $2.6 million.

94

On a personal note, my membership at TPC Potomac at Avenel Farm, which I have had for over twenty-five years, is a true testament to the importance of women owning their own membership. Before the club opened, I presented a non-solicited proposal to the Marketing/Public Relations Director for TCP Avenel Farm to help market the club to women and minorities, which included some lobbyists too. Being a lawyer, the Director recognized the value of lobbyist memberships. He accepted my proposal, and I was successful in selling one of the club's first corporate memberships to a very successful black business owner in Virginia, as well as several other memberships.

This was long before the emergence of Tiger Woods, so it was not an easy sell to get women and minorities to understand the value of this golf facility, especially as it was not yet bricks and mortar, I had just the beautiful brochures to show. I opted not to take my commission for the sales I made, but to use my commission to purchase a membership instead. The Director reminded me that I already had a membership (I was married at the time which allowed me access through my spouse's membership with TPC Sawgrass), but I said it was not *my* membership. I needed my own company membership to be in my name, and the name of my company, under which I was doing business. He accepted, and that was our deal.

Years later, I was divorced, and had I not purchased my own exclusive membership, I no longer would have had access to the club. I have maintained a very active role over the years at my club by hosting the majority of my *The Art of the Deal: Golf–Access to Success* workshop/seminars, hosting many dignitaries and Heads of State, and hosting my clients' families and friends, for graduation parties, corporate board meetings, private dinner

95

parties, and other social activities and, of course, golf. By utilizing my membership in this manner, I continue to expose my guests to a new venue and potentially generate additional business for the club.

WHAT'S YOUR ROI?

This leads to the important question I get: "How do you measure the Return on Investment (ROI), for doing business on the golf course?"

"You measure your ROI the same way you prepare your annual Marketing, Business Development, Social, and Public Relations budgets. You should include business golf as a serious line item and use the club as your place of business."

While I was still in high school (and working), I would travel to a congressional country club on a monthly basis to meet one of our corporate clients in the "men's grill room." There was an exception for me, as a woman, because of our client. Later, I discovered that this client did not play golf at all, he told me "This is where my clients are. I am here everyday to do business over lunch and to play cards." This was his office.

One day I received a telephone call from the CEO of a major defense contracting company to join him and two of his top clients that had just come into town. He asked to set up a game at my country club and needed a fourth. I arrived at the club before his guests to take care of signing them in, pay their fees, reserve a caddy, purchase golf balls and golf caps, and so forth.

At the conclusion of the game and after lunch in the club, the CEO asked me to meet him again later. He wanted to discuss a pending business opportunity and needed my help. The result of that meeting was that he hired me as a Business Development Consultant for corporate accounts. He was a retired military person and the majority of his connections were to the military, and he was only playing golf on military courses. He needed to be introduced to executives at a major oil company I was doing business with. Because I had a business development contract at the club, where I had my membership, I convinced my defense contractor client to purchase a corporate membership to provide him access to the type of business clients he was seeking to make contacts with. He was so pleased, by the return on his investment, that soon after he joined another high-profile country club in the area, and continued to use these memberships for business and social purposes, including hosting his wedding reception at the club.

All of these examples, demonstrate why it is extremely important for you to understand how to use memberships as part of business marketing and development.

⟋⟋⟍⟍

These pages have been written to motivate, and inspire you, to achieve, beyond limitation, through powerful networking and enjoyable experiences. I hope that you have learned, and have been convinced, of the strength and value of golf as a global business tool.

97

GOLF

It is a contest, a duel or a melee, calling for
skill, courage, strategy, and self-control.

It is a test of temper, a trial of honor,
a revealer of character.

It affords the chance to play the man/woman
and act the gentleman or woman.

It includes companionship with friends and
opportunities for courtesy, kindness and
generosity to an opponent.

—The 1995 Crosby—Ten Years in North Carolina

AFTERWORD

I was born in Washington, D.C. From the time I started junior high school, I worked for Harris Electric, a small, neighborhood electrical engineering and contracting company with my brother, Leon, "Sonny," and the boy across the street, Junior Page. There were about 23 male mechanics on staff and the boss' wife, Elena Harris, who really ran the place. We were teenagers and all of the men were much older who played on our bowling team. Every month they bowled against other small companies in our area. I excitedly joined the team along with Sonny and Junior. We were quite good at bowling and our team won the majority of the games.

One day, in the beginning of summer, one of the men from another company asked if I played golf. I knew nothing about golf and responded, "Why?" He said that during the summer they didn't bowl, they played golf. I looked him straight in the eyes and said, "Yes, I can play." He invited us to play golf with them. I felt a little awkward agreeing to a game I had never heard of, but I definitely didn't want to be left out. Immediately returning to the office, I asked Elena what was this game called 'golf.' She said, "Rose, that's what they play at the Congressional Country Club where you have been going every month to meet our client." I often visited this client at the club to bring contracts and collect payments, but I didn't know that it was a golf country club.

Determined not be left out of the summer games, I tried to get my brother and Junior to go with me to learn how to play golf. They weren't interested. Golf was not a game that was popular among kids in my neighborhood.

Golf, over the years, has provided me much pleasure, opened many personal and professional doors of opportunity, and taken me to six continents. I am extremely grateful for all it has given me. Today, in our global society, I don't believe there is a better business tool than golf.

As an African American and a veteran businesswoman in the golf industry with over 30 years of experience, I am a living example of *how* and *why* the game is an important tool for business, global networking, economic development, public relations, sales and marketing, branding, leadership development, and diversity and inclusion. Golf has been and continues to be a tremendous sport for me.

My intention in writing this book was *not* to teach you how to play golf, but to share with you why you should have golf in your portfolio. Through some of my personal "case studies," I have provided real life stories and insights to dispel misconceptions about the game. I especially wanted to respond to and thank the many peer level executives and college students who have attended my *The Art of the Deal: Golf–Access to Success* Workshop/Seminars and repeatedly requested, "Please write a book."

After reading this book, I hope you are encouraged to begin to use the golf course as a new "classroom" and a new "boardroom," a place of respect where you look neither up to or down on anyone—we all walk on the same fairways. Realizing that the golf course is a great place to build relationships and to learn more about your internal, external, and potential clients and co-workers, I hope it becomes the place to bond while mixing business and a great game in a truly sociable atmosphere.

I trust that this book has been educational, inspirational, and motivational enough to get you into the game and to show you that one does not have to be a great golfer to be a great person to play golf with! So I leave you as new ambassadors of the number one global business tool… golf.

I look forward to seeing you at one of the next *The Art of the Deal: Golf–Access to Success* Workshop/Seminars and on the fairways. And always remember, 'Have fun, it's not your day job.'

Yours in golf,

Rose Harper

The Art of the
DEAL:
G⛳LF-
Access to Success

GLOSSARY

There are literally hundreds of golf terminologies. The following is just a sampling of the most commonly used terms.

Ace (Hole-In-One): An ace is a term used to describe a hole-in-one. This means the golfer only took one shot from the tee box to get the ball inside the cup on a given hole.

Approach: A shot hit towards the green (His approach shot to the 17th hole came up short of the green) or towards the hole (Sam Snead was a great approach putter).

Attend the Flag: To hold and then remove the flag while another player putts.

Away: The ball that is the greatest distance from the hole when more than one golfer is playing. It is the first to be played.

Birdie: When a golfer uses one less hit, or stroke, than the par granted to him on any hole. For example, a golfer only took three hits or strokes to put the golf ball into the cup on a par 4 hole.

Bogey: When a golfer takes one more stroke than the par on that hole.

Bunker: A hollow comprised of sand or grass or both that exists as an obstacle and, in some cases, a hazard. (The greens at Winged Foot were protected by deep bunkers).

Caddie: A person hired to carry clubs and provide other assistance. (A good caddie can be worth several strokes a round).

Carry: The distance a ball will fly in the air, usually to carry a hazard or safely reach a target. (Many of the holes at Pine Valley require a substantial carry over waste areas).

Choke Down: The act of gripping down on the shaft, which is generally believed to provide greater control. (She choked down on a 7-iron and hit a beautiful pitch to save par)

Double Bogey: A score of two over par on a hole. (The double bogey ended her hopes of defending her title).

Double Eagle: A score of three under par on a hole. (Gene Sarazen's double eagle at Augusta National is one of the most famous shots in golf history).

Driving Range: Another term for a practice area. Also known as a golf range, practice range or learning center. (Watson headed for the driving range following his round.)

Eagle: A term used to describe the number of shots a golfer took to hit the golf ball into the cup. It means that the golfer used two fewer strokes than par granted him or her. It is commonly seen on par 5 holes. Using three strokes less than the par granted on a hole is commonly called a double-eagle, but in Britain (and some parts of the US) it is referred to as an albatross.

Fairway: A part of a hole that has the shortest grass. It typically runs from the Tee box to the green. The goal of each golfer is the keep the ball in the fairway, because it is the easiest place to hit the ball from.

Golf Range: A facility where people can practice their full swings and, in some cases, their short games. (In Japan, golf ranges are very popular because the number of golf courses is limited).

Grass: Commonly referred to as "turf grass," the grasses used on golf courses are traditionally tough, fast-repairing grasses that can withstand plenty of traffic. Grass on golf courses differs from region to region based on how the grass will stand up to heat or cold. Different grass may also be used on the tee box, fairway and greens.

> **Bermuda Grass:** The main turf choice for golf courses and athletic fields throughout the warmer regions and across the equator.

> **Bent Grass:** A popular low-growing grass that is planted on the greens of the golf course and occasionally on the fairway and tee box areas.

Kentucky Bluegrass: A blue-green grass that can be found in your family's lawn and on most golf course fairways.

Rye Grass: The seeds of this grass germinate quickly and can be used as a temporary ground cover while slower-growing grasses take hold.

St. Augustine Grass: A warm weather grass found primarily along the Southern U.S. coast that can survive in many types of soil.

Zoysia Grass: A warm weather grass from Southeast Asia that grows in many types of soil and can survive droughts.

Green: The green is a circular shaped area where the golfer is trying to reach with his golf ball shots. It is the location that has a flagstick and a cup. The green has the grass cut the shortest from any other place on the golf course. This allows a golfer to easily roll the ball across the green to reach the cup, or hole. Once the golfer gets the golf ball inside the cup, that hole is completed.

Grip: The placing and positioning of the hands on the club. The various types include the Vardon or overlapping, the interlocking and the 10-finger or baseball grip. (The Vardon grip is the most popular grip today). There is also the reverse-overlapping grip, in which the index finger of the left or top hand overlaps the smallest finger of the right or bottom hand. This is primarily used in putting, although some players use this grip when chipping the ball.

Ground: When referred to in the Rules of Golf, it means the point when the club touches the ground (or water) prior to playing the shot. (It is against the Rules of Golf to ground your club in a hazard).

Group Lesson: A teaching session in which several pupils work with one or more PGA Professionals. This type of lesson is particularly effective for beginners, especially juniors. (The PGA of America offered group lessons for youngsters as part of the city's summer recreation program).

Handicap: The number of strokes a player can take off his total score at the end of a round of golf. Each golfer is granted a number of additional strokes, or hits, based on their skill level. A handicap allows golfers of different skill levels to play evenly against each other.

Hazard: Obstacles or obstructions strategically placed on the golf course by the designer of the course to make the game more challenging to play. The different hazards include ponds, lakes, streams, bushes, sand traps, grass bunkers or any other obstacle setting along the sides of each hole and surrounding the green.

Intended Line of Flight: The direction a player plans for his ball to begin after impact. (Because she planned to hit a hook from the tee, her intended line of flight was at the righthand fairway bunker).

Learning Center: A complete practice and instruction facility, which may or may not be on the site of a golf course. (While there was no golf course nearby, she was able to work on her game at the local learning center).

Links: The term for a course built on linksland, which is land reclaimed from the ocean. It is not just another term for a golf course. (The Old Course at St. Andrews is the most famous links in the world.)

Marker: A small object, like a coin, that is used to mark the spot of the ball when it is lifted off the putting green.

Mulligan: The custom of hitting a second ball—without penalty—on a hole, usually the 1st tee. (Mulligans are not allowed according to the Rules of Golf).

Par: The number of strokes, or hits, a golfer is allowed for one particular hole. All of strokes are added up to give the course a total par, such as 70 or 72 for 18 holes. A golfer is said to shoot par if they use the exact number of shots to hit the ball from the tee box and into the cup on the green.

Pitch-and-Run: A shot from around the green, usually with a middle or short iron, where the ball carries in the air for a short distance before running towards the hole. (She played a beautiful pitch-and-run to within a foot of the hole).

Pivot: The rotation of the body around a relatively fixed point, usually the spine. (Throughout his career, people have marveled at Fred Couples' full pivot).

Private Lesson: Generally speaking, when a PGA Professional gives a lesson to a single pupil. (After losing in the club championship, she had a private lesson with her PGA Professional).

Radius: The distance between the center of the swing arc (the target or forward shoulder) and the hands on the grip. (Because of his unusually long arms, his swing had a large radius.)

Raised Swing Center: Elevating the central area in the body (somewhere between the top of the spine and the center of the neck) around which rotation takes place. What the novice frequently refers to as "looking up" and results in a swing that is too high.

Rap: To hit a putt with a short, firm stroke. (Former PGA Champion Gene Sarazen liked to rap his putts).

Reading the Green (or Putt): The entire process involved in judging the break and path of a putt. (Her caddie, Tom, was a genius at reading a green).

Rough: The rough is an area of the golf course that runs along the sides of the fairway and has longer grass.

Round Robin: A tournament format in which players or team play a variety of other teams, the winner being the player or team that accumulates the highest number of points. (The two brothers always teamed in the club's Fall Round Robin).

Sand trap: The common name for a bunker.

Semiprivate Lesson: An instruction format where a limited number of pupils work with a Professional. (When the triplets wanted to take up golf, their parents arranged for them to take semi-private lessons with their PGA Professional).

Stance: The position of the feet at address. (He played most shots from an open stance).

Stroke Play: Also known as medal play, it is a form of competition based on the cumulative number of strokes taken, either over one round or several. (Most professional tournaments are stroke play events).

Sweet Spot: The point on the clubface where, if it is struck with an object, the clubface will not torque or twist to either side. (To find the sweet spot on his putter, he held the grip with his thumb and forefinger and let it hang vertically. Then he tapped the face of the putter with the eraser-end of a pencil until the putter head moved back without any torquing or twisting).

Tee Box: The starting point on each hole where a golfer begins play from.

Unplayable lie: A lie in which the ball is impossible to play such as in a thicket of trees.

Whiff: A complete miss. Also known as an "air ball." (He was so nervous that he whiffed his drive.)

---

http://www.pga.com/golf-instruction/instruction-feature/fundamentals/golf-glossary

http://www.easypars.com/common-golf-terms/

http://www.hittingthegreen.com/common-golf-terms

The Grass Ceiling, Inc.
"Breaking the grass ceiling on the world's golf courses"

Are the *executive women and minorities* in your organization prepared for *growth, advancement,* and *leadership?*

Is your organization looking for an innovative *corporate incentive program* for retention and appreciation of your internal executives and external *clients and associates?*

The Grass Ceiling, Inc., established in 1995, is a global company that has parlayed over 30 years of experience with the golf industry into a series of dynamic workshop/seminars—*The Art of the Deal: Golf–Access to Success.*

These are powerful and comprehensive workshop/seminars designed to empower peer-level *executive women and minorities in government, business, education, and foreign affairs* to navigate the complex world of business relationships within and across genders.

The Art of the Deal: Golf–Access to Success program *is not just another golf school.* It is a business model used to instruct executive women, minorities, and men in the use of golf as of a networking, business, and economic development and leadership tool.

The Grass Ceiling has been a service provider to the sporting industry, offering professional consultation and management advice to executive level women, college-aged youth and minorities. It recognizes that powerful business relationships are cultivated but remain very exclusive, even though educational and career opportunities have created a more diverse portrait of American business. The game of golf can provide a neutral zone to promote effective communication and positive bonding between professionals and their peers. This is particularly true for women and ethnic minorities who have not, historically, participated in the game of golf.

- Works closely with corporations, organizations, colleges, to show women and men how to effectively use the game of golf to enhance business development and relationships.

- Levels the playing field for emerging market groups in preparation for growth, advancement, and leadership opportunities.

- Provides unique programs that are proven vehicles for gaining exposure throughout various industries and among executive peer-level groups.

Benefits: When you attend our workshop/ seminars, you will...

- Invest one day in yourself and gain valuable knowledge and skills you can use for a lifetime.

- Develop an appreciation for this powerful business tool prior to either taking your first lesson or executing your next swing

- Build your confidence to compete by familiarizing you with an understanding of the rules of etiquette and the basics of the game

- Have access to the types of networks that enable you to reap benefits far beyond normal employee contributions

- Receive a Continuing Education Certificate (provided with the comprehensive programs)

Program Overview

Unpressured, informal, business casual, yet intensive, peer-level workshop/seminars. Our workshop/seminars can be specifically designed to meet the client's needs, and can be held at the client's golf club or corporate offices. We offer one to three day educational packages, presented at high-end private golf club facilities, both in the US and South Africa.

- All hands-on instructions are given by certified LPGA/PGA professionals, and a 3 minute video of your basic instructions is yours to take home on a flash drive

- 9 holes of golf are included for those who have golf experience

- Meals and a wrap-up networking cocktail session close out the full day.
- Two/three day comprehensive retreat packages are available

Format
- All programs are offered as lectures
- Half-day sessions
- Full-day workshops
- Developmental retreats
- Partnership intensives.
- Customized to meet your corporate needs and interests
- Access to The Art of the Deal Global Networking Directory, an electronic database (provided in the more comprehensive programs)

Topics
- Basic concepts
- Equipment
- Rules of the game
- Protocols
- Winning strategies for the game
- Tournament play
- Winning strategies for play and business negotiation

Art of the Deal Leadership Programs

The Art of the Deal: Golf is comprised of three unique Executive Development Programs. Each was created to accomplish similar social, personal and professional enhancement objectives among differing groups. Workshops, which require personal instruction, will last for approximately 6-7 hours and accommodate a maximum of 40 participants; seminars can accommodate as many as 250 persons/seminar.

Product Type	Professional Leadership Development Workshop	Executive Peer-Level Workshop/ Seminars	University Lecture Series*
Target Market	Created to accommodate peer-level executives from a variety of backgrounds. In most cases, individuals will enroll in this course for personal and professional enhancement.	Available to corporations, industries and associations desiring to provide content for leadership candidates via an executive development course.	Designed primarily for colleges and universities, providing global networking information and business insight, addressing challenges often encountered in corporate America.
Frequency	A minimum of six workshops will be conducted per year.	A minimum of six workshops will be conducted per year.	A minimum of ten lectures will be conducted per year.

*In 2002, under the direction of Dr. Peggy Berry, Director of Howard University Continuing Education, the course was approved for continuing education credits. This unit was certified by the International Association for Continuing Education and Training (IACET).

ROSE HARPER
Founder & Director

Q.T. JACKSON
Educational Specialist

MAXINE LEGALL
University Professor

NANCY OWENS
Certified Trainer

For additional information on our programs for individuals and special corporate and college packages, please contact us:

THE GRASS CEILING, P.O. Box 5874, Washington, DC 20016
grassc@aol.com | 202.966.5622 | 202.966.5623 FAX
www.thegrassceiling.com

About the author
ROSE HARPER

ROSE *is* an entrepreneur, philanthropist, lecturer, adjunct professor, contributing writer to golf publications, passionate golfer, a born leader and the foremost global golf subject matter expert and related events executive. She is the recipient of countless awards for her lifetime achievements in business, community service, development, and in the field of sports, especially golf. She has established herself as a golf advisor and trainer to U.S. presidents, royalty, celebrities, ambassadors, Fortune 500 CEOs and for the underprivileged all over the US. The key to her success is her sincere yet savvy networking ability, skills that she has embedded in her multilevel *The Art of the Deal: Golf–Access to Success* business workshop/seminars.

Rose's legendary contributions to the Golf Industry include the founding of the PGA Tour Wives Association, initiating the Golf Digest Minority Golf Summit, and the reformatting of the PGA player credentials. She established a minority joint venture golf course design team (Rose Harper, Gary Player & Arnold Palmer) to provide a golf feasibility study for the Nations Capital. She coordinated and implemented a broad range of projects in the public and private sectors. She was the first person of color to operate and manage a professional 18-hole golf complex through the U.S. Department of the Interior. Rose has served on the Board of Directors for the Bing Crosby Golf Tournament. Rose was recognized by the PGA of America as a Player Manager. She organized the first multi-racial sporting event in the history of South Africa; she was a U.S. Delegate to the Seoul Olympics. Her college course on the Business of the Olympics is now taught at George Washington University. She was honored in 2006 by the PGA of America as a founding member of the PGA Minority Collegiate Golf Championship, in 2009 she was inducted into the DC Hall of Fame receiving their Sports Legacy Award, in 2011 she was inducted into the National Black Golf Hall of Fame, and in 2013 she was the first woman to receive The Sam Lacy Pioneer Award.

One of the most important visionary women in the world of golf, Rose Harper has parlayed 30 years of exposure and experience in the sports management and special events industry, and has provided leadership training to build a successful business that adds value to other professionals. Additionally, she served on the D.C. Baseball Commission and developed a documentary on the History of African Americans in Golf. She has served on many boards and commissions and has chaired the $2.5 billion dollar D.C. Retirement Board.

Ms. Harper founded the Grass Ceiling, Inc. in 1995, as a business empowerment firm that specializes in using the game of golf as a platform to help level the playing-field for women and minorities with their counterparts in the business and academic worlds. The game of golf provides a neutral zone to promote effective communication and positive bonding between professionals.

She has received Executive Certificates in the following areas; The Emerging Trustees Congress- New Orleans, Institute for Fiduciary Education- Yale University, Finance- Wharton School of Business, University of Pennsylvania, National Conference on Banking, International Protocol Association and Business Administration-. She has served as an Adjunct Professor in the School of Business and as a college lecturer at many universities.

Also by ROSE HARPER

The Golfer's Cookbook

First edition, 1977, 175 pp. A book of recipes compiled by the author.
Most of the recipes were contributed by golfers or their wives
of the PGA Tour, and the sale of the book benefitted the
non-profit Leadership Academy fund.